MW01469831

# They're Just Teenagers--
# What Do You Expect!

Discovering God's Expectations For You and Your Child

# They're Just Teenagers--
# What Do You Expect?!?

Discovering God's Expectations For You and Your Child

## Margo Hemphill

elife Press
Nashville, Tennessee

THEY'RE JUST TEENAGERS – WHAT DO YOU
EXPECT?!?

Published by eLife Press
A division of eLife Ministries, Inc.

ISBN 0-9769889-2-5

Copyright © 2005, 2007 by Margo Hemphill

All rights reserved. No part of this book may be produced in any form without permission in writing from the publisher, except in the case of brief quotations embodied in critical articles or reviews.

Unless otherwise indicated, Scripture taken from the HOLY BIBLE, NEW INTERNATIONAL VERSION®. Copyright © 1973, 1978, 1984 International Bible Society. Used by permission of Zondervan. All rights reserved.

The "NIV" and "New International Version" trademarks are registered in the United States Patent and Trademark Office by International Bible Society. Use of either trademark requires the permission of International Bible Society.

Also quoted:
*New Revised Standard Version of the Bible,* copyright 1989 by the Division of Christian Education of the National Council of the Churches of Christ in the USA. Used by permission. All rights reserved.

Cover Design by Jessi Easterling and Margo Hemphill

Printed in the United States of America

# ACKNOWLEDGMENTS

Thank you to my friend Diane Roberts, the first to read each chapter upon completion and give me feedback on grammar and content. I did not consider the fact that Diane was at one time the assistant principal at Dave and Luke's school a disqualification.

Thank you to my friend and sister, Laura Moak, for her encouragement during this project. Laura is one of only a few people still living who can attest that the stories herein are accurate and true! I must add that Laura was not necessarily a willing participant in some of the events described.

And most importantly, thank you to my husband and children for allowing me to have so much fun!

# Table of Contents

**INTRODUCTION** ............................................................................. 1

*"For I know the plans I have for you," declares the LORD, "plans to prosper you and not to harm you, plans to give you hope and a future."* [Jeremiah 29:11]

**GOD EXPECTS A RESPONSE** ..................................................... 8

Samuel -- *Then the LORD called Samuel. Samuel answered, "Here I am."* [1 Samuel 3:4]

**GOD EXPECTS OBEDIENCE** ...................................................... 24

Isaac -- *Then God said, "Take your son, you only son, Isaac, whom you love. Go and sacrifice him there as a burnt offering.* [Genesis 22:2]

**GOD EXPECTS CONFIDENCE** .................................................... 42

David -- *David said to Saul, Let no one lose heart on account of this Philistine; your servant will go and fight for him.* [1 Samuel 17:31]

**GOD EXPECTS PATIENCE** ......................................................... 62

Joseph -- *So when the Midianite merchants came by, his brothers pulled Joseph up out of the cistern and sold him.* [Genesis 37:28a]

**GOD EXPECTS PURITY** .............................................................. 93

Daniel -- *But Daniel resolved not to defile himself.* [Daniel 1:8a]

**GOD EXPECTS DEVOTION** ....................................................... 119

Solomon -- *And you, my son Solomon, acknowledge the God of your father, and serve him with wholehearted devotion ...* [1 Chronicles 28:9a]

**GOD EXPECTS SUBMISSION** .................................................... 139

Mary -- *I am the Lord's servant, Mary answered. May it be to me as you have said.* [Luke 1:38]

**GOD EXPECTS COMMITMENT** ................................................ 163

Jesus -- *Didn't you know I had to be in my Father's house?* [Luke 2:49b]

**GOD EXPECTS ACTION** ............................................................ 184

*I will give them singleness of heart and action, so that they will always fear me for their own good and the good of their children after me.* [Jeremiah 32:39]

# Introduction

*"For I know the plans I have for you," declares the LORD, "plans to prosper you and not to harm you, plans to give you hope and a future."* [Jeremiah 29:11]

For eight years the enemy (parental lingo for teenagers) has surrounded me! Consequently, I have developed some very definite opinions about raising children.

My primary qualification as an expert on child rearing comes from having given birth to three adorable babies, and, subsequently, surviving the ordeal of having each of them metamorphose into teenagers.

Until now, I have been disinclined to share my opinions with anyone outside my immediate family. My hesitancy is not born out of some misplaced feelings of inadequacy, for I am not only surviving this ordeal, I am thriving in what many experts believe to be a hostile environment. Nor do I hesitate because I believe there is a standard of greater value than that on which my opinions are based. Rather, I hedge because this business of child rearing is not as difficult as the recognized experts in the field would have us believe.

Was that a cyclonic wind which passed by my elbows as your mouth flew open in disbelief over my first printed observation about child rearing? If so, you can now understand my hesitancy. However, before you brand me a rebel, please give me the opportunity to make my point.

Yes, I believe that rearing children is only one degree of difficulty greater than keeping a pair of socks mated through three successive launderings. For some of us, this probably makes child rearing just a tad more complicated that what NASA went through to put a man on the moon.

However, indulge me and I will show you not only how to keep that pair of socks mated, but also how to keep them in *your* sock drawer and off *your* teenager's feet.

> As Christian parents we must be learners, as well as teachers.

As Christians, we know that God has a better plan for our lives than we could ever dream up for ourselves. We must take the time to learn what God expects from us and then act according to those expectations. As we do we will grow in the LORD, and as we grow we will be equipped to teach our children. Let me be quick to say, this teaching must not be postponed until our children are teenagers. It must begin when they are in the cradle.

Without our guidance, our children may never know there exists a much higher authority to which they should answer. It is through us that they can experience the joy that comes in knowing and meeting God's expectations.

All parents hope for the same result in child rearing. Whether we name it success, achievement, goodness, kindness, compassion, intelligence, or give it an even more glamorous title, we all desire that our children be *Godly*.

> As Christian parents we desire that our children develop Godly character.

My husband's father was a worker of wood. I have seen him take unsightly pieces of wood and somewhere deep within that stump or log, he discovered an object of beauty and worth.

I have watched him spend hours on delicate carvings, taking care with the most intricate details, knowing that one slip of the blade could mean disaster. In all the hours I watched him as he worked, not one time did I see him try to make a cut or a shave in the wood without having the correct knife. He knew from experience that without the right tool, he would never achieve the look or the feel he wanted from the wood.

From my father-in-law, I learned that there are two requirements essential for producing a beautiful wood carving.

First, you must have a clear understanding of what you want that drab piece of wood to become. You must take that piece of wood and hold it up to the light. You must examine it, you must evaluate it, and then you must envision what can come from that rough piece of beauty.

Once you have decided upon the outcome, you must then acquire the tools to extract from that wood the object of beauty you see within it.

If either of these steps is overlooked, the end result will be less than what you had hoped for.

▼ ▼ ▼ ▶ ▼ ▼ ▼ ◀ ▼ ▼ ▼ ▶ ▼ ▼ ▼

As we waited for our first child to be born, my husband and I knew that buried deep within us was some instinct that would at least see us through the birth and the bonding. Therefore, we were not concerned about our ability, or lack of ability, to parent.

However, I did not realize how strong this parental instinct is until I watched my husband hold our daughter for the first time.

I spied anxiously as he lifted our new baby girl up to the light so he could examine her more closely.

With love in his eyes, he turned her from side to side. He peeked behind her ears; he caressed her eyelids; and he kissed her toes. As he nuzzled her neck, he proclaimed her to be perfect in every way.

Holding our precious gift for the first time, he did the same thing the wood carver does with his piece of wood. My husband examined his child; he evaluated her; and then he envisioned what would come from that tiny piece of raw beauty.

Without even knowing it, he had met the first requirement for raising a *Godly* child.

> As Christian parents we need to adopt God's expectations for our lives and teach our children to do the same.

In acquiring any skill, having the correct tools is essential, and, because raising children is a skill, we must utilize the exact tools needed for the job.

A critical mistake some parents make is to believe they can do their job without these tools. These are the parents who think morals and values are instilled in their children through some osmotic freak of nature. It is these parents who believe that good kids happen by accident and, often, it is too late when they realize their mistake.

Others, knowing the necessity of having the right tools, make the wrong choices. They look to the trends and fads our society has developed as the latest panacea for child rearing.

These parents spend millions of dollars and thousands of hours reading, studying, and seeking the opinions of men. These are the parents whose main focus in life becomes their greatest disappointment when they realize it was not man's opinion that mattered.

If we are to successfully accomplish this goal of raising Godly children, we are left with only one option. We must seek out the set of tools that were developed specifically for accomplishing the task which lies before us. Because we have determined our desired outcome, we need the tools to make it happen. We need the set of standards which have stood the test of time and proven their validity with ongoing success. We need the right tools. We need to know God's expectations for our children. In equipping ourselves with God's plan, we have the tools necessary to raise Godly children.

> We, as Christian parents, must take seriously the responsibility of teaching our children.

James had it right when he said, *"Do not merely listen to the word, and so deceive yourselves. Do what it says."* [James 1:22 NIV]

Knowing God's plan is not enough. We must act on what we know. I can find no Biblical evidence that anyone other than the parent is ultimately responsible for the training of the child. Nor do I find that as parents we have the right to delegate any of that responsibility to anyone or anything else.

It is not enough to know. We must take the time to learn what God expects from us and then act according to those expectations.

Until we take action, we are only fooling ourselves. Believe me when I say, *Our friends are not fooled.* They see the lack of discipline and caring in our children's attitudes. They see very clearly the outcome produced by ignoring God's expectations for our children.

*Our parents are not fooled.* They are merely baffled about how, over the course of one or two generations, such a gradual change in attitude and approach toward our children could produce so dramatic an effect.

Finally, *our children are not fooled.* They know that things should be different, but they have no experience from which to draw in order to change.

We are the only people who are fooled!

I believe that my grandparents were part of the last generation who, as a whole, understood the value of God's standards for raising their children. I believe that somewhere between their generation and mine, the swing toward parenting by default has taken its toll.

As a result, my generation has become the last of a legacy. We are the final source of hope for our children. Without us, our children may never grasp the fact that God places expectations upon them.

We are the bridge between God's plan and the world. We have a responsibility to nurture our children by God's design, not just for their sakes, but for the sake of the generations that will follow them.

We hold in our hands tomorrow's leaders and we will decide whether they will grow in the nurture and admonition of the LORD or wither due to our neglect.

If we are to be successful in passing on God's plan to our children, we must begin now. As Christians, our first step must be to discover God's tools for doing our job correctly.

We need to know what God expects from our teenagers. As we uncover God's desires, God will help us teach our children.

It is important to recognize the truth that God has no expectation from the child or teen that He does not first expect from the parent. As parents, God wants our attention first in order to equip us to teach our children.

We will explore nine of God's basic expectations of us and of our children. We will do this by examining the lives of several Bible characters who exemplify these expectations - in their youth!

These expectations are:
1. **Response** (Samuel): The *boy* Samuel ministered before the LORD under Eli. 1 Samuel 3:1a NIV
2. **Obedience** (Isaac): Abraham said to his servants, "Stay here ... while I and the *boy* go over there. Genesis 22:5 NIV
3. **Confidence** (David): Goliath looked David over and saw that he was only a *boy*. 1 Samuel 17:42 NIV
4. **Patience** (Joseph): Joseph, *a young man* of seventeen, was tending the flocks with his brothers. Genesis 37:2 NIV
5. **Purity** (Daniel): ...*young men* without any physical defect ...Daniel, Hananiah, Mishael and Azariah. Daniel 1: 4, 6 NIV
6. **Devotion** (Solomon): My son Solomon, the one whom God has chosen, is *young and inexperienced.* 1 Chronicles 29: 1 NIV
7. **Submission** (Mary): The *virgin*'s name was Mary. Luke 1:27 NIV
8. **Commitment** (Jesus): When Jesus was *twelve years old*, they went up to the Feast...Luke 2:42 NIV

A ninth expectation - **action** - places *you* in the center of the examination!

May God bless us as we explore together what God's expectations are of us, of our children, and of our teens!

# Chapter One

## God Expects a Response
### Samuel

*Then the LORD called Samuel. Samuel answered, "Here I am."* [1 Samuel 3:4]

My husband, Tommy Hemphill, believes listening is the most important part of any discussion. He has tried to help our children to develop their communication skills by always requiring their attention before he speaks. However, gaining their attention is often more easily desired than accomplished.

Sometimes he employs an appropriately timed *"harrumph"*. You know that trick. It is the little throat clearing technique that has nothing at all to do with a mucous-free air passage. Any dad worth his salt has honed this ploy to perfection.

Tommy has also used the quick snap of the fingers or a prolonged silence coupled with a stern fatherly stare. Whatever the technique, his ultimate goal had always been to gain the undivided attention of our children so that they will listen to him and then give an appropriate response.

It took one ride with K'Anna behind the wheel for Tommy to begin to question his long held beliefs about the process of communicating with a teenager.

K'Anna had been a licensed driver for about three months - long enough to think she was invincible behind the wheel. Because her territory was limited to the area inside a triangle formed by school, Wendy's, and home, she had done most of her driving on four streets. The constraints we had placed on her had not deterred her enthusiasm. What she lacked in variety, she made up in volume. In one thirty day period, she made the trek between our house and school no less than two hundred times.

The familiarity she acquired with the territory did not breed contempt. It bred speed! As her proficiency on the street between home and school increased, the time it took for her to cover the distance decreased proportionally. By the time she learned to take the curve in front of the church on two wheels, her father innocently asked her for a ride to the neighborhood ball park. I was certain Tommy would never have gotten into the car with K'Anna had he been aware of her potential. I stood silently by as the pair pulled out of our driveway.

Trouble began to brew before the two were out of my sight. Less than two hundred yards from our house, Tommy glanced at the speedometer and calmly said, "K'Anna, you need to slow down." He expected K'Anna to listen, understand, and then give an appropriate response to his request.

K'Anna wanted to please her father and eased off the gas enough to make him believe she had every intention of complying with his wishes. But in a moment she had picked up speed again. Just as they were getting ready to top the first hill,

Tommy knew he must intervene before the car took flight. He cleared his throat and spoke more sternly than before. "K'Anna, I said, 'slow down'!"

K'Anna responded immediately, slowing the car to just under the speed limit. With a sigh that revealed her displeasure at being reigned in by her dad, she maintained a moderate rate of speed for a few miles. Lulled by her obvious acquiescence, Tommy was caught unaware when for the third time he noticed their speed had crept back up to the danger zone.

Tommy was angered less by her heavy foot than by her obvious attempt to ignore his warnings. He pushed himself up in his seat and with a near shout said, "K'Anna, slow this car down! This is the last time I am going to tell you."

K'Anna reacted immediately, not by slowing down, but by giving her dad a lesson in communication he would not soon forget. Apparently relieved to hear her father proclaim his intention never again to tell her to slow down, K'Anna adjusted her grip on the wheel, leaned slightly forward, and, with a quick glance at her dad, said, "Good!"

> Can you think of a time in your child's life when you tried to elicit a response? What was the desired result? What was the actual result? Why do you think it is important that children learn to respond - to parents - to others in places of authority - and ultimately, to God.?

## Samuel Responded to God

For many years Hannah was unable to have children. Every year she went with her husband to sacrifice to the LORD God at Shiloh. Every year she prayed and cried out to God to give her a child. She became so downhearted over her inability to conceive that she cried for days, doing without food as she grieved. Then one year she made a vow to God.

*"O LORD Almighty, if you will only look upon your servant's misery and remember me, and not forget your servant but give her a son, then I will give him to the LORD for all the days of his life..."* [1 Samuel 1:11]

The LORD heard Hannah's prayer. She conceived and gave birth to a son.

*She named him Samuel, saying, "Because I asked the LORD for him."* [1 Samuel 1:20b]

Remembering her promise to the LORD, Hannah took Samuel to the House of the LORD at Shiloh when he was about four years old. After she presented him to God, she left Samuel at Shiloh with Eli the priest. Under Eli's tutelage, Samuel grew in stature and in favor with the LORD and with men.

> Sometimes we fail to respond to the voice of God because we are ignorant and inexperienced.

Sometime later, as Samuel was lying down in the temple of the LORD one night, God spoke to him, but Samuel did not recognize God's voice. Thinking it was Eli who had called to him, Samuel immediately ran to Eli and said,

*"Here I am. You called me."* [1 Samuel 3:5a]

What happened to Samuel? How did he respond? In order to answer these questions, recall the circumstances of his upbringing. Samuel was from a good family who worshiped God. He moved into the church when he was four and had lived continuously at the church for about nine years, under the daily guidance of Eli, the priest. Then God spoke directly to him for the first time.

Hannah's son had spent his entire life without any of the outside influences we deal with today. He had no radios, televisions, or computers to distract his attention from God's work. Hannah had dedicated her son to God as a child, and he had spent his life learning how to serve God. If there was ever a teen who had been prepared to hear and recognize the voice of God, it was Samuel.

Yet when God spoke, Samuel did not know God's voice. Confused, he went to Eli and told him what had happened. Eli turned Samuel away with, *"I did not call; go back and lie down."* [1 Samuel 3:5b]

Back in bed, Samuel heard the LORD call again, *"Samuel."*

Repeating his previous action, Samuel returned to Eli and said, *"Here I am; you called me."* But Eli responded, *"My son, I did not call; go back and lie down."* [1 Samuel 3:6]

While it is clear from the Scripture that Samuel had no idea God was speaking to him, it is equally clear that Samuel was justified in his ignorance.

*"Now Samuel did not yet know the LORD: The Word of the LORD had not yet been revealed to Samuel."* [1 Samuel 3:7]

| Sometimes we fail to respond to the voice of God because we are confused. |
|---|

One of the most comforting moments of my spiritual growth came the day I realized that nothing ever occurs to God. Think of the many times you have been in a situation in which you tried to make a competent decision. Suddenly, a new aspect of your circumstance occurred to you. New light dawned and you were able to clearly see the big picture. Wasn't that a wonderful feeling?

Well, that never happens to God because He already knows everything. He already sees the big picture and more.

Confusion is not possible with God. As a Christian, I find solace in the fact that God is not pacing back and forth trying to decide what to do. My faith, my hope, and my life are all in the hands of the One whose decisions have already been made; and all His decisions have been made in my favor.

Samuel, however, was the epitome of confusion. He reacted in the same manner we often react when we are faced with a confusing situation. He made the choice of default. Samuel, in his confusion, assumed it was Eli calling him, because from his perspective, Eli was the only available option.

> Sometimes we fail to respond to the voice of God because we do not understand the revelation of God's Word.

From June, 1974, through July, 1981, I worked at an office complex very near my home. Each day for seven years I traveled the same route to work. Each morning I left my home at 7:35 a.m. and arrived at my office fifteen minutes later.

Upon leaving my driveway, I proceeded two miles, made a right turn, continued two more miles, and turned right again. After another mile, I went through one stop sign and then turned right into the office complex.

At the stop sign each day, I watched as other commuters made the choice to turn left and go up the entrance ramp to Interstate 55. Without fail, I always chose to proceed through the stop sign and remain on the service road to my office building.

I once calculated that during my seven year tenure on this job, I made this same choice over one thousand, eight hundred times.

In 1981, I changed jobs and went to work for a company on the other side of our city. My route to work likewise changed. I no longer traveled the service road, but took a completely different route, entering the interstate very near my home.

One September morning in 1996, more than fifteen years after changing jobs, I noticed a sign had been posted to indicate my regular route was closed for repair. A detour was in order. Very quickly, I made the decision to take the right turn I had taken each morning all those years previous. I remembered that by making one left turn at the stop sign, I would be on the interstate.

Having plotted the detour in my mind, my thoughts turned to the realization that God's desire for me is that I learn to evaluate my circumstances in light of the new truths I learn from Him each day. Placing truth upon truth offers new perspective, new insight in even the most trying situations.

Comfortable in my oblivion, I reached the familiar stop sign where a left turn was needed to complete my detour and get me back on track. I did not make that turn, however. Like Samuel, I made the choice of default. I went straight through the intersection, never giving a second thought to my actions. I took the path of greatest familiarity. Without giving the slightest heed to my other options, I headed straight for a job I had not held for almost fifteen years. Immediately God helped me realize the application of His truth in my situation.

> Sometimes we fail to respond to the voice of God because we lack the correct perspective to make appropriate decisions.

As we seek God daily through prayer and Bible study, God reveals His truths to us, thereby changing our perspective to be more aligned with His.

With each revelation of truth, our options change and expand. As our circumstances change and we are faced with the necessity of choices, we must learn to make our decisions based, not on the default values we acquired at some point in our past, but rather on our cumulative knowledge of God's expectations of us. We must learn to take advantage of our new perspective. Otherwise, we rob ourselves of the joy of spiritual growth. By relying only on judgment by default, we become increasingly confused and disoriented as our circumstances become more difficult to unravel. This myopic viewpoint causes us to miss our turn and subsequently, we are faced with the consequences of poor choices.

For me, getting back on track to work that September morning was an uncomplicated task. I simply continued to the next entrance ramp and gained access to the Interstate.

> For our instruction, God puts people into our lives to teach us and we are to respond to that teaching.

Life is not always as easy as finding the next entrance ramp. Because we often need divine direction to get back on tract, God puts people in our lives through whom He gives us instruction. To Samuel, God gave Eli.

Because God wanted Samuel's attention, as well as, an appropriate response from him, God did what only God can do. He used Eli to help Samuel understand that it was God who called him.

*The LORD called Samuel a third time, and Samuel got up and went to Eli and said, "Here I am; you called me." Then Eli realized that the LORD was calling the boy. So Eli told Samuel, "Go and lie down, and if he calls you, say, 'Speak, LORD, for your servant is listening." [1 Samuel 3:8]*

Did you see it? Did you see the Word of the LORD as it was revealed to Samuel? Did you see how God used Eli to instruct this teenager on the subject of hearing and responding to the voice of God? Did you see how Samuel's confusion was resolved through God's revelation? Without this revelation from God, Samuel could not know that it was God who called him. For Samuel to move on to the next phase of his upbringing, the next phase of his spiritual growth, he had to grasp the concept that God wanted to speak to him and God expected an appropriate response from him. This is exactly what the LORD taught Samuel through Eli.

> Can you recall a time when you learned something through the assistance of another person? As parents, we are often the primary instrument through which God speaks to our children. Can you think of a time when you were that instrument to your child?

God's revelation of Himself is a step that cannot be overlooked as our children learn to be attentive to the LORD. As they understand their need to listen for the voice of God and then respond to that voice, God will choose a suitable means of revealing Himself to them.

Why does God desire to reveal Himself to any one of us, particularly to one of our teenagers? It is very simple. God wants to teach our teenagers His truths to give them the basis for making the right choices in their lives.

Wait a minute. I know what you are thinking.

"My teenager is having enough trouble with the revelation of fifth period math. How will he ever catch on to a revelation from God?"

"Why, he's not sure if a sine is something he's supposed to calculate for an angle or hold up at a pep rally."

"To my teenager, cosine is an action by his parents that simply means he will be driving a new truck this fall."

"And tangent? Why that's something his mother gets on

every time he tries to explain how football is more important than passing some silly French test."

"There is no way under the stars he could possibly catch on to the revelation of the Word of the LORD!"

Well, guess what, my friend. Samuel understood God's revelation of truth, and so will your teenager.

Please, believe me when I say to you, "God wants your teenager's undivided attention. God wants to reveal Himself to your child. And if necessary, God will persistently call until your child answers!"

*So Samuel went and lay down in his place. The LORD came and stood there, calling as at the other times, "Samuel! Samuel!" Then Samuel said, "Speak, for your servant is listening." And the LORD said to Samuel: "See, I am about to do something in Israel that will make the ears of everyone who hears it tingle." [1 Samuel 3:8-11]*

| When we listen, God will make Himself clear. |

When I realized that God wanted the full attention of my three children and that He meant for them to recognize His voice, I thought, "What on earth would Almighty God want to say to my three teenagers?"

For a fleeting moment I hoped the revelation would be something along these lines: "Cleanliness is next to Godliness, so do something about that space you call your room!"

Very quickly, I realized the sanitary condition of my children's bedrooms was probably not very high on God's list of priorities.

As I began to digest the scope of God's truth in this matter, I soon realized just how high a priority God places on that moment in our lives when we first recognize His voice.

God had a definite reason for wanting Samuel's attention

just as He has a definite reason for wanting your child's attention. God wanted Samuel to be able to recognize His *voice* because a time would come when Samuel would need to know God's *heart*. In knowing God's voice and learning God's heart, Samuel would one day point out God's choice for political leadership to the nation of Israel. What is more important, this appointed ruler would establish the house and lineage from which our Savior, Jesus of Nazareth, would come.

After that first encounter with God, Samuel continued through the years to listen for and respond to the voice of the LORD.

▼ ▼ ▼ ▶ ▼ ▼ ▼ ◀ ▼ ▼ ▼ ▶ ▼ ▼ ▼

Many years later, when Samuel, now old, was the spiritual leader of the Israelites and their judge, God again spoke to him.

Through the years, Samuel had seen his people rise up against God's authority. He had seen those same people demand that a king be anointed as their leader. At God's direction Samuel had anointed Saul as the first king of Israel. Samuel was directly involved in Saul's reign as mentor and advisor. He watched as Saul rejected God's authority and as Saul was rejected by God. Through all of these spiritual and political changes, and the subsequent turmoil they produced, Samuel remained true to the LORD.

It was while Samuel was mourning the condition of the people and their leader that God spoke to him again.

*The LORD said to Samuel, "How long will you mourn for Saul, since I have rejected him as king over Israel? Fill your horn with oil and be on your way; I am sending you to Jesse of Bethlehem. I have chosen one of his sons to be king."* [1 Samuel 16:1]

As I studied this portion of Scripture, I came to have a new appreciation for the sovereignty of God. Samuel had known for quite some time that, because of Saul's disobedience, God had selected a replacement.

*"You acted foolishly," Samuel said. "You have not kept the command the LORD your God gave you; if you had, he would have established your kingdom over Israel for all time. But now your kingdom will not endure; the LORD has sought out a man after his own heart and appointed him leader of his people, because you have not kept the LORD's command."* [1 Samuel 13:13-14]

Even though it was at the request of the people that God had originally given the nation of Israel a king, God's purposes would prevail even when the leader was disobedient. The LORD desired a king for Israel who would be a man after God's own heart. Because Saul had chosen to ignore God's commands, God, in His sovereignty, ordained that another would take his place.

Samuel's ability to listen for and respond to the voice of God would now be integral in selecting the new leader of God's people. The lessons learned as a teen would now effect the outcome of a nation. As God's representative, Samuel would need to hear, understand, and respond to God's direction in anointing Saul's replacement.

With clear instructions from the LORD, Samuel traveled to Bethlehem to anoint the new king. When he arrived, he assembled Jesse's family for a worship service. It was during this service that God would point out His choice to Samuel. Remember that Samuel did not know which of Jesse's sons had been divinely chosen. Samuel had simply been instructed to go to Jesse of Bethlehem because God had chosen *one* of his sons to be king.

*When they arrived, Samuel saw Eliab and thought, "Surely the LORD's anointed stands here before the LORD."* [1 Samuel 16:6]

> When we respond to the Lord, He will help us make wise choices.

This was a natural assumption on Samuel's part. Being the oldest of eight sons, Eliab certainly must have had an air of authority about him. I am sure he had developed considerable leadership skills just from having to contend with so many younger brothers. I am also confident, based on Samuel's immediate reaction to him, that Eliab was probably in excellent physical condition, tall, handsome, articulate, and in every manner a real man. A specimen fit to be king.

*But the LORD said to Samuel, "Do not consider his appearance or his height, for I have rejected him. The LORD does not look at the things man looks at. Man looks at the outward appearance, but the LORD looks at the heart."* [1 Samuel 16:7]

How many times have you made this same mistake? Don't be afraid to admit it. We have a tendency to make choices based on outward appearances. It is apparent from the Scriptures that this man of God shared that proclivity. What Samuel did not do, however, was allow his error in judgment to deter him from his mission. On the contrary, he became even more determined to point out God's selection. So, in spite of Eliab's qualifications for the position, and without regard to his obvious good looks, Samuel responded to God's rejection of Eliab, as he did to the other sons of Jesse.

*Then Jesse called Abinadab and had him pass in front of*

*Samuel. But Samuel said, "The LORD has not chosen this one either." Jesse then had Shammah pass by, but Samuel said, "Nor has the LORD chosen this one."* [1 Samuel 16:8-10]

And so it continued. Jesse paraded seven of his eight sons in front of Samuel. Jesse must have begun to panic when he realized he was running out of sons and God's anointed had yet to be found.

*Samuel said to him, "The LORD has not chosen these."* [1 Samuel 16:10b]

You must appreciate the faith Samuel displayed in God's ability to reveal the truth. From all outward appearances, Samuel had viewed all of the candidates for the job. He had considered all the options. Because God had yet to make a selection, however, Samuel was faced with a dilemma. Israel had no king and Samuel had no prospect. It was at this point that Samuel did something I consider quite profound -- he assumed there had to be more choices. Samuel placed complete faith in God's Word as God had revealed it to him.

*So he asked Jesse, "Are these all the sons you have?" "There is still the youngest," Jesse answered, "but he is tending the sheep." Samuel said, "Send for him; we will not sit down until he arrives."* [1 Samuel 16:11]

Jesse's hesitancy to call David in from the field revealed his exclusion of David as a possibility, but Samuel would not be discouraged. Samuel expected God to provide a king and God was prepared to accommodate him.

Because Samuel was faithful to God's instructions, God accomplished what He had promised.

*So he sent and had him brought in. He was ruddy, with*

21

*a fine appearance and handsome features. Then the LORD said, "Rise and anoint him; he is the one." So Samuel took the horn of oil and anointed him in the presence of his brothers, and from that day on the Spirit of the LORD came upon David in power.* [1 Samuel 16:12-13]

> Why does making the correct response to God sometimes take patience? What things in our lives and in the lives of our children make responding to God difficult?

Samuel provides a powerful picture of the kind of adult God expects your child to become. How much more could we possibly desire for our teen than that he learn to listen for God's voice and then respond with the confidence of knowing that God will make Himself clear and will reveal His purposes?

How much more could we want than a child who learns to settle for nothing less than God's best and then has the staying power to wait on God, to stand firm, and be confident that God will provide?

Parents, God wants to speak to your child. Godly living is based upon the foundation of hearing and understanding God. Teach your child to listen and respond to God's voice so that when the time comes, your teen will be prepared to make the right choice. When this moment arrives, let nothing interfere with your child's ability to respond. Help your child prepare to choose God's *heart.*

**Parent to Teenager**: To respond to God, Samuel had to know who He was. Eli was God's instrument to teach Samuel that the Lord was calling him to make a personal response. Samuel responded, "Speak, Lord, for your servant is listening." The LORD calls you by name and wants you to recognize Him as the LORD of your life, and yourself as His servant. This is the most important response of your life.

## Rules to follow:

After inviting Him into your life as your Lord and Savior, determine to always respond to His will for your life.

Search the Scriptures and discover how you must respond in each circumstance of your life.

Listen when God speaks to you through the voice of another - your parents, your minister, your teacher - or someone else of His choosing.

Remember that God is never confused and that He always gives clear instructions.

Father,

Help me learn to listen for Your voice. Help me learn to respond to you in the way that you desire. As I learn, help me teach my child what You expect of him. Help my child understand how to listen for Your voice and respond to Your heart.

# Chapter Two

## God Expects Obedience
### Isaac

*Then God said, "Take your son, you only son, Isaac, whom you love. Go and sacrifice him there as a burnt offering.* [Genesis 22:2]

    For many years our family has been a part of a hunting club in Jasper County, Mississippi. King's Flat, so named for the plantation which once operated on the same plot of land, was established by a group of men whose main desire was to have a family oriented hunting club. Each of these men had, at different times, been associated with other hunting clubs through the Southeast. Not one of these associations had offered its members what this group of men wanted most--a chance to enjoy, with their families, their chosen sport. The commitment by the membership to encourage the entire family's participation was the one thing that drew my husband to this club in the early 1970's. He knew the time would come when he would want to share this experience with me and with our children.

On Wednesday, the last week of November, 1986, as had become our custom over the previous twelve years, our entire family gathered at the hunting club for our Thanksgiving celebration.

By nine o'clock that night Tommy's patience with our three children had almost found its limit. Our youngest, Luke, only a few weeks shy of his fifth birthday, had spent the entire day on a personal mission to unravel his father's last nerve.

The problems had begun early that morning when Luke refused to wear socks to school. Because Tommy has eternally held to the belief that obedience and respect are two of the first concepts a child should learn, he could not forego this opportunity to use Luke's stubbornness as a perfect occasion to teach these values.

Following the teaching methods to which he clings, Tommy gave Luke one chance, and one chance only, to right the wrong. When Luke chose to ignore this fine episode of graciousness on his father's part, he sustained a swat to his backside which my husband hoped would help him understand that obedience and respect were both expected and required. As we would learn later that night, this lesson was not completely lost on Luke.

Our children's bedtime was nine o'clock. We held to this rule even when we were away from home so that our routine did not become disrupted beyond repair. Being at the hunting club was not cause for exception. At 9:00 p.m., Tommy climbed up to the loft of our cabin where our three children were playing. After giving each a kiss, he called for lights out. This declaration of day's end was gratefully accepted by our two older children. K'Anna and Dave were very soon settled and asleep. For Luke, however, Dad's command for quiet became cause for revolt.

When, after thirty minutes, Luke was still talking to the shadows, my husband cleared his throat, and, in his deepest, most authoritative voice, said, "LUKE!"

At that moment, my expectation was that Luke would recognize the severity of his father's tone and would respond by quietly slipping into his bed and off to sleep. I truly believed the end to this day had finally arrived. How wrong can a mother be about her child?

Not only did Luke respond, he responded in like manner! "WHAT?!" Luke answered in a tone laced with the implication that he was not happy about being disturbed.

As the realization of what had just occurred began to sink in, Tommy and I both glanced up toward the loft to see Luke standing at the top of the stairs. With his best impression of George Patton, there he stood with his hands on his hips and his feet slightly apart, anticipating the forthcoming response from his father. Somewhere in the distance, I could faintly hear the words of the late General as he said, "We shall attack and attack until we are exhausted, and then we shall attack again."

Astutely assessing that the battle for obedience might be waning in Luke's favor, my husband decided to take tactical advantage of the situation by trying to catch the enemy off guard. Quickly suppressing the laugh that the sight of this little general invoked, Tommy did the only thing he could think to do. He stood; then he looked straight into Luke's eyes and said, "When you address me, son, you will do so with respect! It is 'SIR' to you, young man!"

Drawing himself up to his full height, using the most convincing voice, and with a snapped salute, Luke immediately responded, "WHAT?! SIR!"

Looking back, we realize that however clouded his judgment, Luke did begin on that fateful evening to conceive the importance of obedience and respect. For Luke, this episode became the foundation for understanding a part of God's expectations for him.

## Isaac Obeyed His Father

Although the story recorded in Genesis 14 is the story of Abraham's obedience to God, it is necessary to pause a moment to underscore the absolutely unwavering and unquestioning obedience which Isaac, Abraham's young son of promise, gave to his father, Abraham.

The point must be made that Isaac was obedient to *his* father because Abraham set before him the example of being obedient to *his* father, the LORD God. Everything then that can be said of Abraham, can likewise be said of his son, Isaac.

> Our obedience to God is a measure of our respect for Him.

Since the beginning of time, obedience has been a device used by God as a measure of our respect for Him. It is a perfect gauge, since it is our nature as human beings to be obedient to those whom we hold in high regard. Even though our obedience to God is for our own benefit, it is also the best way we have to worship and honor Him. For this reason, God expects obedience from us and from our children.

In the Garden of Eden, God gave Adam and Eve access to every abundance with only one exception, the Tree of Knowledge of Good and Evil. Because they were overcome with desire for this one prohibited item, Adam and Eve were driven to dishonor God and, through their disobedience, to be separated from God. Disobedience did not preclude Adam and Eve from having God's love; but it did keep them from having God's best. Disobedience robbed them both of the delight of being in God's presence and learning to worship Him properly.

> Obedience to God allows us to participate with Him as He completes His plan.

God expects obedience from our children. God wants our children to spend time in his presence. Our children need to comprehend that God desires and deserves their worship. They need to learn that obedience to God's commands is the key to worship. As their parents, it is we who have the responsibility to teach our children these truths.

▼▼▼▶▼▼▼◀▼▼▼▶▼▼▼

Abraham was a man who loved and respected God. From this love and respect grew Abraham's faith that God could be trusted to act according to His Word.

*The LORD said to Abram, "Leave your country, your people and your father's household and go to the land I will show you. I will make you into a great nation and I will bless you; I will make your name great, and you will be a blessing. I will bless those who bless you, and whoever curses you I will curse; and all peoples on earth will be blessed through you."* [Genesis 12:1-3]

Let's study this picture for a moment. In these few sentences, God promised this seventy-five year old man (and his sixty-five year old wife) that He would make a great nation of him. All Abraham had to do was pack, leave his father's house and move to a new country.

Before we go any further, it is important to note that, at this point in their lives, Abraham and Sarah were childless. To become a great nation, it was critical that they have at least one heir. Therefore, it would be understandable had Abraham questioned God's promise. Abraham, however, did not question His promise because Abraham's faith did not rest in what he could accomplish, but in what God would accomplish.

Let's try for a moment to put ourselves in Abraham's shoes. Since Abraham would live another 100 years, he was young at 75. He and his wife had established a home in Haran where he was probably quite satisfied with his accommodations and his life there. Most likely, the last thing on his mind was packing up his family and moving to a new home. I am sure that under different circumstances, had the thought of relocating occurred to him, it would certainly not have included a move to a country he had never seen.

In Abraham's response to God's promise, we find a very important truth which we will discuss later in detail: God's perspective and man's perspective are worlds apart. Because Abraham chose to see his circumstances from God's perspective, he was able to leave the familiar and move toward the unknown with the confidence of knowing that God would be true to His Word.

*So Abraham left, as the LORD had told him; and Lot went with him. Abram was seventy-five years old when he set out from Haran.* [Genesis 12:4]

Abraham went to the land God showed him. When he arrived in Canaan, the LORD reconfirmed His promise of blessings to Abraham.

*The LORD appeared to Abraham and said, "To your offspring I will give this land." So he built an altar there to the LORD who had appeared to him.* [Genesis 12:7]

Through the years, God reaffirmed His promise to Abraham. When Abraham proposed to God that because Sarah was barren, his servant, Eliezer, could be his heir, God remained steadfast in His promise.

*Then the word of the LORD came to him: "This man will not be your heir, but a son coming from your own body will be your heir." He took him outside and said, "Look up at the heavens and count the stars -- if indeed you can count them." Then he said to him, "So shall your offspring be."* [Genesis 15:4-5]

When Sarah tried to do God's job by giving her maid, Hagar, to Abraham for the purpose of producing an heir, God remained true to His Word.

*Then God said, "...but your wife Sarah will bear you a son, and you will call him Isaac."* [Genesis 17:19a]

Even as Sarah laughed at the possibility that she might have a child in her old age, God patiently renewed His promise.

*"Is anything too hard for the LORD? I will return to you at the appointed time next year and Sarah will have a son."* [Genesis 18:14]

Never let anyone tell you that God's timing is anything less than perfect. Twenty-five years had come and gone since God's first proclamation of promise to Abraham. At ninety, Sarah was not just a little over the hill; at best, she was forty years past child bearing age. Had there been a medical journal in publication at the time, I am sure a pregnant Sarah would have made the cover. The caption might have read: **Once Again, The God of Abraham Accomplishes the Impossible**.

God made happen what He had promised, and He did it in a manner whereby no man could doubt His intervention. With one promise fulfilled, God established His control over nature, His sovereignty over man, and His desire to bring man back into his presence. Under any other circumstances, one might be able to conclude that Isaac's birth was something other than an act of God. God left no doubt.

Even though the Scripture does not indulge us with the details of Isaac's childhood, I am sure Abraham must have shared with his son the circumstances surrounding his birth and God's promise that through him, Abraham's offspring would be too numerous to count. I am equally certain that Abraham's complete trust in God's Word gave Isaac the assurance of knowing that God would see his promise to completion.

Through Abraham, Isaac had a personal perspective of how obedience to God was necessary for God to receive the honor, the glory, and the worship He deserves.

> Obedience to God does not demand our best; obedience to God demands our all!

It was after Isaac had entered his teens that his ultimate lesson in obedience came. Isaac had grown up watching his father offer up the best animals of their herds in sacrifice to God. I am sure he understood that God expected and deserved the best he and his father had to offer. The concept of giving one's best to God was not new to Isaac, but giving one's best was not the lesson in obedience that Isaac would learn that day.

The time had come for Isaac to learn the lesson we all must come to understand. God wants more than our best. God wants everything. To truly honor and worship God in a manner which pleases Him, we must be prepared to sacrifice everything! We must be willing to put everything we have on God's altar.

*Some time later God tested Abraham. He said to him, "Abraham!" "Here I am," he replied. Then God said, "Take your son, you only son, Isaac, whom you love, and go to the region of Moriah. Sacrifice him there as a burnt offering on one of the mountains I will tell you about."* [Genesis 22:1]

As a parent, my heart breaks every time I consider what must have gone through Abraham's mind when God gave these instructions. Put aside for a moment the fact that Abraham knew Isaac was a miracle from God, given for a specific purpose. Neither consider Abraham's commitment to trust God for all things. Think only about the personal feelings which must have coursed through Abraham's body.

Isaac was Abraham and Sarah's baby, their little boy. Think of the memories which must have flooded Abraham's mind. How many times as a toddler had Isaac held out his arms to his daddy to be held? How often as a child had Isaac run after Abraham, trying to keep in step with his father? How many hours had Abraham spent teaching his son about God's love and faithfulness only to have it all culminate with God's command to offer Isaac as sacrifice?

Even though the questions about what God told him to do must have seemed endless, for Abraham there was only one answer -- obedience.

*Early the next morning Abraham got up and saddled his donkey. He took with him two of his servants and his son Isaac. When he had cut enough wood for the burnt offering, he set out for the place God had told him about.* [Genesis 22:3]

As on previous occasions, Isaac accompanied his father to make the sacrifice. When they had walked three days, Abraham saw the place where God wanted the sacrifice to be made. Through the instructions Abraham gave to his servants we are able to peer into an open window as we examine Abraham's unwavering trust in God.

*He said to his servants, "Stay here with the donkey while I and the boy go over there. We will worship and then we will come back to you.* [Genesis 22:5, emphasis mine]

If there is one word which can best describe Abraham's attitude at this juncture of his life, it is confidence. Abraham knew that to obey God would mean death for his own son. But Abraham knew with even greater certainty that God would honor His Word.

Because God had promised that a nation would be established through Isaac, and because Abraham believed God would faithfully execute His promise, Abraham did not hesitate to carry out God's command to sacrifice Isaac.

Abraham was confident that if God required Isaac's death, then even more God would require Isaac's resurrection from death. Abraham expressed no doubt when he gave his servants their instructions. Abraham knew that both he and Isaac would return.

It is obvious from the Scripture that Isaac was clueless about the role he would play in the worship service. His mind was busy with common details as, in typical teenage fashion, he pointed out his father's deficiencies for the sacrifice.

*Abraham took the wood for the burnt offering and placed it on his son Isaac, and he himself carried the fire and the knife. As the two of them went on together, Isaac spoke up and said to his father Abraham, "Father?" "Yes, my son?" Abraham replied. "The fire and wood are here," Isaac said, "but where is the lamb for the burnt offering?"* [Genesis 22:6-7]

Whether it was Abraham's purpose to draw Isaac's thoughts away from the reality before them, or simply to reassure Isaac of God's control over their lives, is not clear from Abraham's answer. It is clear, however, that Abraham had no intention of allowing anyone or anything the opportunity to impede his progress toward obedience.

*Abraham answered, "God himself will provide the lamb for the burnt offering, my son." And the two of them went on together.* [Genesis 22:8]

I can imagine that the remainder of their journey must have been made in silence. Abraham surely spent his time reflecting on God's direction and intervention in his life. He may have even recalled the memories of God's promise as a way to salve his heart with the assurance of God's faithfulness. Isaac, oblivious to the requirement being made of his father, probably kept a keen eye out for the offering that God would provide. Each in the silence of his own thoughts, the two -- father and son -- traveled until they came to the place God had appointed.

*When they reached the place God had told them about, Abraham built an altar there and arranged the wood on it. He bound his son Isaac and laid him on the altar, on top of the wood.* [Genesis 22:9]

How God's heart must have suffered as He looked forward in time and saw the day when His own son would become the final sacrifice. As Abraham bound Isaac's hands and feet, God must have envisioned the leather bindings that would secure Jesus on that fateful Friday to come. When Abraham, with quiet resolve, placed Isaac atop the wood which would very soon be consumed by the sacrificial fire, God must have seen Jesus as He would one day willingly lie down on the wooden cross, to be nailed securely in place, awaiting His destiny.

Even as Isaac, with no sign of contention, prepared to draw his final breath, God's heart must have broken in anticipation of that moment in the future when His own Son, without struggle, would yield His life in complete obedience to the Father's plan.

*Then he reached out his hand and took the knife to slay his son. But the angel of the LORD called out to him from heaven, "Abraham! Abraham!" "Here I am," he replied. "Do not lay a hand on the boy," he said. "Do not do anything to him. Now I know that you fear God, because you have not withheld from me your son, your only son."* [Genesis 22:10-12]

> Obedience to God is better than sacrifice to God.

By staying the sacrifice at this moment of completion, God uncovered for us a wonderful facet of His character. God has priorities. There are some things which are more important to God than others.ABraham found that in God's list of priorities, obedience has a higher place than sacrifice.

For some of you this revelation will not take on its highest meaning until you comprehend that in having priorities, God has order. It is through this order that God cares for us, teaches us, sustains us, and loves us. Through obedience to God, we become part of that order.

Does God expect obedience from your teenager? Absolutely. Through obedience to God, your teen becomes part of God's order. Through obedience your teen will nurture his relationship with God and develop the total level of commitment that God requires. Through obedience, your teen will be blessed with God's best for his life and for his family. Through obedience, your child will learn to subordinate his will to the Will of God, yielding himself as a suitable offering unto the LORD. Through obedience, your child will honor God with the highest form of praise.

And through obedience your child will become the recipient of God's provisions.

*Abraham looked up and there in a thicket he saw a ram caught by its horns. He went over and took the ram and sacrificed it as a burnt offering instead of his son. So Abraham called that place The LORD Will Provide. And to this day it is said, "On the mountain of the LORD it will be provided."*

[Genesis 22:13-14]

God provided a sacrificial ram that day, but God's provisions did not end there. Through the years God continued to bless Abraham. His flocks and herds increased along with his silver and gold. Abraham prospered as he continued to serve God.

*The LORD, the God of Heaven, who brought me out of my father's household and my native land and who spoke to me and promised me an oath, saying, "To your offspring I will give this land" -- He will send His angel before you so that you can get a wife for my son from there.* [Genesis 24:7]

> Obedience to God by the parents influences other members of the household.

Though God's provisions were many, one promise had yet to be fulfilled. Isaac was still without a wife and children.

The time finally came for Isaac to be married. As was the custom in his day, Abraham was responsible for securing a mate for his son. Because Abraham wanted God's best, he put the choice in God's hands. Abraham sent Eliezer, his chief servant, back to his own family to find a wife for Isaac. In his directive to Eliezer to find a wife for Isaac, Abraham made it clear that God's intervention was to be expected.

Before you panic, let me assure you that I am not promoting arranged marriages. Finding a husband for my daughter or wives for my two sons is the last thing I would want to take on in my old age. I do believe, however, that God has a vested interest in my children's futures and He has made arrangements for their mates. Let me show you why I believe God is in the divine match-making business.

Eliezer traveled until he reached the town of Nahor in Abraham's homeland. He stopped on the outskirts of town near a well. It was evening when he arrived and Eliezer knew that this was the time of day when the women would come out to the well to draw water. What happened next is a testament to Abraham's faithfulness to God. Eliezer prayed to the God of Abraham for success in finding the right girl for Isaac.

Because Eliezer had been in Abraham's household for many years, he was aware of his master's dependence on God's leadership. Eliezer knew from experience that God claimed an active role in the lives of Abraham and Isaac. Eliezer knew also that God's role was not limited to the big ticket events, but also infiltrated even the smallest facet of their lives.

For this reason, Eliezer saw his part in this mission, not as the decision maker, but simply as God's messenger. Eliezer knew his job was to serve as temporary liaison between Isaac and the woman that God had chosen for his wife. Eliezer continued to pray.

*May it be that when I say to a girl, 'Please let down your jar that I may have a drink,' and she says, 'Drink, and I'll water your camels too' -- let her be the one you have chosen for your servant Isaac. By this I will know that you have shown kindness to my master.* [Genesis 24:14]

Clearly, Eliezer was not testing God's ability or desire to provide a mate for Isaac. Eliezer had been by Abraham's side for many years and was certainly aware of God's plans for Isaac. Eliezer knew that God had revealed His special plan to Abraham more than twenty-five years before Isaac's birth. By outlining this scheme for recognition, Eliezer was merely confirming with God a method by which he could know God's choice. A simple means to avoid an error.

As things turned out, before Eliezer could finish his prayer, God's choice appeared at the well. Rebekah was very beautiful and pure. Her servant's heart became evident when she not only gave Eliezer a drink, but she offered to draw water for his camels as well. Eliezer watched very closely to determine if she was the one God had chosen. When Rebekah had done all the things Eliezer had prayed for, one last question remained.

You will remember that Abraham's instructions to Eliezer included the stipulation that Isaac's wife should come from Abraham's own people. Because Eliezer had yet to determine Rebekah's parentage, he was not completely sure that Rebekah was God's choice. I believe, however, that Eliezer's trust in God's sovereignty was evident in the way he phrased his next question.

*Then he asked, "Whose daughter are you? Please tell me, is there room in your father's house for us to spend the night?"* [Genesis 24:23]

Eliezer had asked of Rebekah the mandatory question about her parentage. But before Rebekah could answer, Eliezer asked permission to spend time with her family. Because visiting with Rebekah's family was necessary only if she was God's choice for Isaac's bride, Eliezer had given himself away with his question.

Eliezer's assumption proved correct when Rebekah answered that she was the daughter of Bethuel, the son of Nahor. Well, what do you know about that! Rebekah was the granddaughter of Abraham's brother. The last requirement had been met. Eliezer had traveled all that distance and the first place he stopped after arriving in Abraham's homeland occasioned his meeting a member of his master's family. Rebekah was Abraham's grandniece. Coincidence could never produce so precise an outcome. Do you understand now why I say that God is in the match-making business?

After explaining his mission to Rebekah's father, Eliezer and Rebekah headed for home.

*But he said to them, "Do not detain me, now that the*

*LORD has granted success to my journey. Send me on my way so I may go to my master."* [Genesis 24:56]

Meanwhile, Isaac was at home mourning the death of his mother. One evening, as he went out into the field to meditate, he looked up to see Eliezer and Rebekah approaching. For any of you who believe that someone other than God would be more suited in choosing your child's partner, watch what happens next.

*Rebekah also looked up and saw Isaac. She got down from her camel and asked the servant, "Who is that man in the field coming to meet us?" "He is my master," the servant answered. So she took her veil and covered herself. Then the servant told Isaac what he had done. Isaac brought her into the tent of his mother Sarah, and he married Rebekah. So she became his wife, and he loved her; and Isaac was comforted after his mother's death.* [Genesis 24:64-67]

Notice that God's choice for Isaac was exactly what Isaac needed. Isaac and Rebekah were completely compatible, a perfect match. Isaac had no complaints about the woman God had chosen for him. He loved her and was comforted by her. Why? Because, through His sovereignty, God had made Isaac and Rebekah especially for each other. No trial period was necessary for this couple. They were perfect for each other. Once again, God became the LORD Who Provides.

Through the years, both the servant and the son had observed the obedience of the father. Because of Abraham's example, Eliezer and Isaac knew that God's provision waits on the other side of obedience.

Obedience is required if your child wants God's blessings. If you have any doubt about what you may expect, let me assure you that during the process of exacting obedience from your child, God will carry him to the mountain. There will be occasions when, as his parent, you will be required to lead him.

When that time comes, do not waver in your own resolve to obey God. Help your teen find the strength to say "Yes" to God when every fiber of his being is screaming "NO!"

Give your teen a reason to depend on God. With your own submission to God's commands, let your teen see in you that God's provisions will always be waiting for him on the other side of obedience.

Understand that God wants to be involved in every facet of your child's life. Help your child seek God and strive to be obedient to His every command. In doing so, help him enjoy God's best for a lifetime.

**Parent to Teenager**: I realize my awesome responsibility to obey God. Only through obedience to Him can I expect to set the example for you to follow. As I exact obedience from you, so does He exact obedience from me - and also from you. When I obey God I am at peace and my life is productive because He knows what is best for me. I can trust Him never to misguide me. I will sincerely try to be the kind of parent who gives godly leadership to you. As I expect you to obey me, I want to teach you by example that God also expects you to obey Him. His Word is written for your edification. Study the Scriptures and obey His Word.

## Rules to follow:

Say 'yes' to God and bring good and not evil into your life.

Be confident in God's Word and obey what it says.

Know that obedience is more important to God than sacrifice.

Obey your parents and those who have jurisdiction over your life. In doing so, your heart is prepared for obeying God when He speaks to you.

Obey because God requires you to obey. To do otherwise is to invite disaster into your life.

Father,
Help me learn to be obedient to you. As I learn, help me to teach my child. Give me strength to march resolutely toward your desire for my life. Help me gain confidence as I await your provisions. Give me courage, Father, to trust You for all my needs as I lead my child to your altar for worship.

# Chapter Three

## God Expects Confidence
### David

*David said to Saul, Let no one lose heart on account of this Philistine; your servant will go and fight for him.*
[1 Samuel 17:31]

December comes to Mississippi in many different ways. At times, the gentleness of her presence is deceiving with warm days and comfortable nights. At other times, her winds rage through the warmth of unseasonable temperatures provoking vicious thunderstorms which rock and roll through our peaceful landscape. During these periods of nature's wrath, we gentler folk often bear witness to brilliant displays of electrical energy as the power generated by the thunderstorm discharges to ground.

Then, there are those times when December brings with

her the harsh cold of a northern winter. Freezing rain, ice, sleet, and occasionally snow crash down on a mild southern climate. Left in their wakes are downed power lines, immobilized motorists, and surprised grocers unprepared for the onslaught of shoppers motivated by a forthcoming period of freezing temperatures.

Try as I might, I will never comprehend that unnamed force inside a Southerner that sends his body into a feeding frenzy at the mention of a hard freeze. You can recognize this condition from the piercing stare caused by a brain that has decelerated to an activity level just short of comatose. I have seen good, decent people face off on aisle three over the last can of dark red kidney beans simply because some weather forecaster predicted a possibility of snow flurries. It is a most unusual phenomenon with all systems returning to normal when temperatures again rise above the freezing mark.

If you live north of the Mason Dixon Line, please try to evaluate the Southerner's reaction to cold weather with at least a modicum of compassion. We recognize a tire chain only from the description found in our Sears catalog; and we believe snow plows and snow blowers have sustenance only in the mind of some northern entrepreneur. Out of habit, we expect only the mildest of winters and are usually caught by surprise when the Northern express pays a visit.

It was a mild period of weather that escorted the Hemphill family into our new home. December arrived before our second week in the new house was complete and table talk quickly turned to preparations for the Christmas season. Because our house is two-storied, the first item of business was to determine how many additional lights would be required for a proper Christmas display. Let me explain that the word "proper", when used by our family in this context, means a degree of illumination that, when viewed from sub-orbital space, would be capable of confusing a spy satellite. I'm talking about a beacon in the cosmos.

After we agreed on the number of new lights and our list for other decorations was completed, I was given the task of purchasing all the required items. When I delivered the goods the following afternoon, my job was finished. I was assured my assistance would not be needed for the planning or the implementation of the Christmas lighting project. Our illumination specialist, K'Anna, had her crew of two conscripted and ready for service. With the lights in hand, the three immediately retired upstairs to plan their attack.

Later that evening, Tommy and I watched the local weather report and discovered that a cold front was moving through the Dallas, Texas area. True to form, this northern blast was going to bring sub-freezing temperatures, ice, and sleet. If the weatherman could be trusted, the front would be in our area by morning and overnight the temperatures would plummet fifty degrees.

Just as predicted, we awoke the next morning to find a blanket of ice covering our neighborhood. The children's thoughts turned to their lighting project since all county schools were temporarily closed due to inclement weather. This was to be expected, since in Mississippi any precipitation not expressly in liquid form warrants a school closing.

Tommy and I readied for work after cautioning our children to use care as they hung the Christmas decorations. Undaunted by our concern, K'Anna assured us that at sixteen, she was quite capable of overseeing her two younger brothers for the day.

I smiled as I considered how mature she had become in the previous few months. I was pleased to see her display of confidence as she resolved to see this project accomplished.

By mid-morning the blanket of ice had begun to melt. Before afternoon arrived, the ice had disappeared completely from all areas of direct sunlight.

It was this warming trend that enticed the lighting crew to set about the task of hanging the Christmas lights.

So that the import of the events I am about to describe does not escape you, let me mention two significant facts. First, the windows on the top floor of our home are approximately sixteen feet from the ground. Second, Dave outweighed K'Anna by at least ten pounds.

Even though our home is positioned several hundred feet from the street, it is clearly visible during the winter months. That same evening, as I topped the hill approaching our driveway, I looked through bare limbs to see a mass of light hovering about our house. The brilliance was formed from pinpoints of light escaping every available square inch on the exterior of our home. At 5:30 p.m., with dusk falling across the hillside, the glory of my children's efforts shone radiantly into the universe. The Hemphill home heralded the beginning of the Christmas season.

It was after I turned into the drive and approached my house that I realized the project was not complete. What I witnessed next induced my right foot to jerk involuntarily, sending my knee on a collision course with my mouth. Then, just as suddenly, that same foot slammed the brakes with such force the frame of my car shook as it ground to a halt.

There, sixteen feet above the ground, was Dave hanging head first from an upstairs window. Out of the corner of my eye I saw Luke directly below Dave with his arms extended as though prepared for an inevitable rescue attempt.

And leaning through the upstairs window, with a confidence that comes from misplaced authority, was the miscreant responsible for this catastrophe. With her toes hooked on the inside edge of the window frame, K'Anna was holding Dave with one hand on each ankle as he attempted to secure the final string of Christmas lights.

The potential outcome of the situation exploded in my brain just as my feet hit the ground. When I threw my hands up and tried to scream, I caught sight of K'Anna's eyes. Deep within those blue pools of confidence, I saw the reflection of my twelve-year-old son poised for a death spiral. One slip of the wrist and he would be a crumpled heap at my feet. When I searched K'Anna's expression, however, I saw no evidence that the severity of this situation had even begun to penetrate the thick surface below her blond mane.

My fear and uncertainly must have registered with K'Anna at that moment. In an attempt to assuage my fears and convey the level of confidence she felt in her ability to safely hold her brother on the brink of disaster, she sent a smile in my direction. This was not just any smile, mind you. What she gave me was a brilliant, nothing-but-teeth, I'm in control and can do anything, smile.

Then immediately, she contradicted her smile of promise by releasing Dave's right foot. This action yanked Dave sideways causing him to pivot around the one stronghold his sister still had on his left ankle. As his body rotated, the string of lights was snatched from his grip.

While I waited in stunned disbelief, expecting Dave to follow that string of lights to the ground, K'Anna raised the hand she had freed, calmly waved to me, and said, "Don't worry, Mom. I have everything under control."

> Think about areas of your life in which you place your confidence in other people. Have there been times when this confidence was misplaced? What about times when this confidence was rewarded?

## David Knew In Whom to Place His Confidence

The ability to be confident or to have confidence is a natural progression of our emotional and spiritual development. Through the process of maturation, we rely on our relationships to help form the foundation on which we build a system of trust. Many times, however, we go awry by trusting someone or something without proper cause. In doing so, we open ourselves up for heartache and disappointment. However, we can always be confident when we place our lives in God's hand.

Saul was the king of Israel. Due to Saul's disobedience to God's commands, he had been rejected by God. David was anointed by Samuel to replace Saul, but it would be quite some time before the change in regimes would occur.

At the time of David's anointing, the Spirit of the LORD left Saul and God allowed an evil spirit to torment him. Saul's servants suggested that he search for someone to play the harp, reasoning that the music would soothe Saul when the evil spirit was upon him. With Saul's assent, one of his servants mentioned a possible candidate for the job.

*One of the servants answered, "I have seen a son of Jesse of Bethlehem who knows how to play the harp. He is a brave man and a warrior. He speaks well and is a fine-looking man. And the LORD is with him."* [1 Samuel 16:18]

Consider for a moment the impression this young man had obviously made on Saul's servant. Notice the list of qualifications entered on David's behalf.

First, he was a musician whose talent had been noticed by the king's court. Remember, these servants were trying to soothe their king and it was in their best interest to find someone who could do the job well. Only a musician of exceptional talent would have suited.

Second, David was already known for his bravery and his ability as a warrior. As a shepherd of his father's herds, David had often successfully defended the sheep against attacks by wild animals.

Third, David was articulate and very handsome. Both traits would be beneficial as David performed his service to the king.

The most important qualification David had, however,

was listed last. The LORD was with him.

David was obviously qualified for the job of musician in Saul's court. But court musician was not the job for which David had been anointed. David was to be the king. God had ordained that David would rule the nation of Israel and when God's timing was right, David needed to be prepared to step into his position.

As qualified as David was for the job of musician, he was sorely deficient in the qualifications needed in a king. As the youngest of eight brothers, David's opportunities to hone his leadership skills were probably nonexistent. Growing up in a household as the baby of the family is difficult under any circumstance. Constantly answering to any one of seven older brothers, however, probably left David with no time for anything other than staying alive and out of trouble.

Because he was the shepherd in the family, I am sure he had little or no training in the financial end of his family's business. His responsibilities kept him out in the pasture with the flocks, not at home with the books. David was also probably unfamiliar with the hierarchical system needed to make a monarchy run smoothly. But in spite of all his obvious shortcomings, he would be king. He had been anointed by God to lead the nation. And the LORD was with him.

*Then Saul sent messengers to Jesse and said, "Send me your son David, who is with the sheep." So Jesse took a donkey loaded with bread, a skin of wine and a young goat and sent them with his son David to Saul.* [1 Samuel 16:19-20]

I never cease to be amazed at God's resourcefulness when it is time to put a plan into action. By God's hand, Saul found himself in need of a musician to serve in his court. God then arranged for an eloquent resume to be entered on David's behalf. By asking for David, Saul was unwittingly used of God to introduce his successor to the nation of Israel. Through divine arrangement, David obtained personal training in his areas of deficiency, training Saul unknowingly made available.

David's list of qualifications would soon transition from shepherd to leader. Soon he would be fit for the king he would become. God would use the rejected leader to present his anointed replacement. This would be accomplished without David having to submit an application. God's plan was in action.

Remember, David knew he was God's choice for Saul's replacement, but he did not know when his ascension to the throne would take place. David knew only to trust God's heart and seek to serve Him. He knew the day would come when he would be called on to take his position of authority.

> As we submit to God's leadership in our lives and He begins to show us the plans He has for us, how willing are we to accept God's way, as well as His outcome?

When David was finally summoned to the king's court, it was not to be king, but to perform the duties of a servant. When the messenger arrived to take him back to Saul, David discovered he was to serve, not to be served. Imagine his surprise! But David continued to trust God. He knew God's plan for him and he was confident that in God's time that plan would come to fruition.

What a powerful lesson is found in these few verses of Scripture. David knew he was king, yet he had to spend time as a servant before he could claim that position.

Always remember that through holiness, God is complete. In keeping with this facet of His character, God never plots an end without a means. God's programs are comprehensive. God never determines an outcome without first ordering each and every step required to attain the outcome.

Sometimes we must wait. Sometimes we must serve. Sometimes we must be a servant while we are waiting to be a king.

David was no exception. God put David into a position to learn the ins and outs of the operation of a nation while serving Saul as court musician and David did his job well.

*Then Saul sent word to Jesse, saying, "Allow David to remain in my service, for I am pleased with him."* [1 Samuel 16:22]

Some time later, when David was back home with Jesse and the sheep, the Philistines gathered their forces to make war on the Israelites. When Saul got wind of the Philistine muster, he positioned his troops along a hill opposite the Philistines. The Valley of Elah spanned the distance between the two armies.

It was not uncommon in David's day for issues of war to be settled between two champions, one each to represent the two opposing armies. Therefore, no one was taken by surprise when the Philistine's champion stepped forward to offer his challenge. What did give rise to a shock wave of terror that rumbled through the Israelite camp was the size of the giant. Goliath of Gath was six cubits and a span in height. That's Hebrew for nine feet, ten inches tall. Even Saul, who was a full head taller than all the other Israelites, must have paled in comparison to Goliath. [See 1 Samuel 9:2]

In order to get a clear picture of Goliath's size, travel by imagination to your local school gymnasium. Look down under the ten foot goal and see Shaquille O'Neal standing at attention. Give particular regard to his size. At seven feet, one inch and three hundred and ten pounds, Shaq is massive. As he raises his hands to grab the net, realize there is little more than fifteen inches between the top of his head and the bottom of the net. His arms are huge and his chest expansive. He exudes strength.

Now glance across at the gym door. Watch as Goliath of

Gath enters the gym. Notice that Goliath is almost three feet taller than Shaq and at least one hundred and twenty-five pounds heavier. Make note of the way his head barely clears the rim when he passes under the goal. Watch as he extends his right arm perpendicularly, holding his hand palm down. Mark the distance between the top of Shaq's head and the bottom of Goliath's hand. Can you believe it is more than twelve inches? Do you get this picture? Can you even comprehend the size of this giant who was prepared to champion the Philistines?

Not only was Goliath massive, he bore armor and weapons which matched his girth. For his head he had a helmet and for his body, a coat. Covering the front of his shins and thighs were leggings. Each piece of Goliath's armor was structured from bronze plate which, even though more malleable and less dense than iron, was still quite heavy. His total suit weighed over one hundred and twenty-five pounds. Strapped to his back was a bronze javelin. The spear which he carried in his hand had an iron point weighing fifteen pounds. Imagine giving that a hurl! Every muscle in Goliath's body must have been honed to perfection just from the daily strain of bearing the weight of all that metal garb. In a word, Goliath was immense. He was a phenomenal specimen built for battle -- a lean, mean, fighting machine.

*Goliath stood and shouted to the ranks of Israel, "Why do you come out and line up for battle? Am I not a Philistine, and are you not the servants of Saul? Choose a man and have him come down to me. If he is able to fight and kill me, we will become your subjects; but if I overcome him and kill him, you will become our subjects and serve us." Then the Philistine said, "This day I defy the ranks of Israel! Give me a man and let us fight each other." On hearing the Philistine's words, Saul and all the Israelites were dismayed and terrified.* [1 Samuel 17:8-11]

Saul's men were afraid of Goliath. They shook with fear

as they listened to the challenge issued by the giant. These were the same Israelite warriors who had defeated the Philistine army at Micmash Pass. This was the battle in which Saul's son, Jonathan, along with his armor bearer prepared to invade a Philistine encampment. Before they climbed the cliff up to the encampment, they agreed that a specific response from the Philistines would be their sign of God's deliverance. As Jonathan and his armor bearer climbed the cliff, the Philistine's noticed their approach and called out for them to come on up. This was the sign. God would give the Philistines into their hands.

In that first attack, these two warriors killed some twenty Philistine soldiers encamped in an area of about half an acre. God then caused a panic among the entire Philistine army. The Scripture describes what was probably an earthquake uniquely situated under the Philistine forces. When Saul mustered his men to attack, they found the Philistine army in complete confusion, striking each other with their swords.

*So the LORD rescued Israel that day ...* [1 Samuel 14:22a]

## Misplaced confidence leads to disaster.

What had changed since the battle at Micmash Pass? Was it the presence of Goliath or something more? Why was Saul's army now afraid of the same men they had so convincingly routed at Micmash Pass? The same army, the same enemy, the same cause -- what had changed?

Only one thing had changed. God was no longer the object of the Israelite army's confidence. At Micmash Pass, the Israelites were the armies of the LORD. Their confidence was in God's ability to defeat the Philistines. They had the security of knowing that their trust had not been misplaced. And God did not disappoint them. Through divine intervention He rescued

His people.

Now this same Israelite army was at the Valley of Elah. Once again they were facing the Philistines. This time, however, their confidence was not in God, but in Saul. Even Goliath recognized their situation when he asked them,

>...*and are you not the servants of Saul?* [1 Samuel 17:8c]

> Confidence placed in God gives us the victory.

Do you see the difference? When the Israelites put their confidence in what God would do, they were successful. They were able to accomplish things which appeared to fall outside the realm of possibility. However, when they put their confidence in Saul and began to consider what he could do, they shook with fear because the deficiency was evident. Through their misplaced confidence the Israelites were poised for defeat.

▼▼▼▶▼▼▼◀◀▼▼▼▶▼▼▼

For forty days, Goliath stepped out each morning and each evening to issue his challenge. For forty days, the armies of Saul cowered in fear.

David's three oldest brothers were with Saul out at the battle front. David had remained with his father at Bethlehem taking care of the sheep. Like any good father, Jesse was concerned about the well-being of his children. He was anxious to know the status of Eliab, Abinadab, and Shammah. With supplies of grain, bread, and cheese, Jesse sent David out to the battle lines to bring back some word of assurance about his boys.

David arrived at the front to find his brothers lined up with the other Israelite warriors. As he was talking to them, the Philistine giant stepped out, and as had become his custom, shouted his defiance. David heard it and saw his own protectors cringe in fear. As David plied the men around him with questions, he revealed his own correct understanding of God's expectation of confidence.

*David asked the men standing near him, "What will be done for the man who kills this Philistine and removes this disgrace from Israel? Who is this uncircumcised Philistine that he should defy the armies of the living God?"* [1 Samuel 17:26]

David's perspective was completely different than that of his countrymen. When David viewed the Israelite troops he saw them correctly as the armies of the living God. When his countrymen considered their own station, they were the servants of Saul. David expected the giant to be defeated by only one man, but Saul's army shook with fear each time they were threatened by one man. Goliath had defied the armies of the living God and David knew that God was prepared to deal with the insult. David's trust did not lie with men, but with the LORD God of Israel. David's confidence was correctly placed. Saul's confidence was not. What a difference existed between the two.

When Eliab heard David's questions, he burned with anger against his youngest brother. He accused David of having a wicked heart. He even charged David with conceit. David reacted in a normal teenage fashion.

*"Now what have I done?" said David. "Can't I even speak?"* [1 Samuel 17:29]

David seemed oblivious to the fact that the entire Israelite army held an opinion completely opposite his own.

David's comments about the Philistine were reported to Saul. When Saul sent for David to be brought before him, the conversation between the teenager and the king could have been the origin of the saying, "out of the mouths of babes".

Confidence in God produced the winning perspective.

*David said to Saul, "Let no one lose heart on account of this Philistine; your servant will go and fight him."*
*Saul replied, "You are not able to go out against this Philistine and fight him; you are only a boy, and he has been a fighting man from his youth."*
*But David said to Saul, "Your servant has been keeping his father's sheep. When a lion or a bear came and carried off a sheep from the flock, I went after it, struck it and rescued the sheep from its mouth. When it turned on me, I seized it by its hair, struck it and killed it. Your servant has killed both the lion and the bear; this uncircumcised Philistine will be like one of them, because he has defied the armies of the living God. The LORD who delivered me from the paw of the lion and the paw of the bear will also deliver me from the hand of this Philistine."*
*Saul said to David, "Go, and the LORD be with you."* [1 Samuel 17:32-37]

Even with Saul's attempt to dishearten him, David would not be dissuaded. He displayed a total trust in God as he answered Saul's concerns about his age. David knew that because his confidence was in God's ability to perform, his age had no bearing on the situation. In less than two minutes of conversation, David convinced Saul that the problem was not the one giant Philistine, but rather Saul's lack of confidence in God's ability to deliver his people through one man.

> Confidence in God grows as we view our circumstances from God's perspective.

David taught Saul that being confident in God requires viewing your circumstances from God's perspective. Goliath of Gath had defied the armies of the living God. From God's perspective, that insult could not be excused. David pointed out God's intervention each of the previous times he had faced a foe much larger than himself. David correctly placed Goliath in the same category as the lion and the bear: They were all opportunities for God to reward David's confidence in Him.

So, Saul gave his permission for David to fight the giant. However, when he made David dress in his armor, it was clear Saul was still unable to view the situation through God's eyes. Instead he continued to see things from his own perspective.

David protested.

*"I cannot go in these, because I am not used to them." So he took them off.* [1 Samuel 7:39b]

God uses what a person knows, what he has, and what he has experienced to strengthen his confidence.

In giving your teenager opportunities to exercise his confidence, the LORD will put before him situations which seem impossible at first glance.

If there is a second truth in the account of David and Goliath which will give your child an advantage it is this: God will never send your teenager to do a job wherein his current abilities and current knowledge are not sufficient. Your teen's confidence in God's ability to make him successful, coupled with what he knows and what he has, will always be enough to get the job done. Watch as David proves this truth.

*Then he took his staff in his hand, chose five smooth stones from the stream, put them in the pouch of his shepherd's bag and, with his sling in his hand, approached the Philistine.* [1 Samuel 17:40]

Did David stop by the bookstore and pick up a "how-to" book on killing giants? No. Did he borrow his brother's sword or use Saul's shield? No. Did he buy a warrior's leather pouch to hold his sling and pebbles? No. What did David do? He took only those things he was accustomed to using: his shepherd's pouch, a sling, and five smooth stones from the stream. Even though these items were all unconventional when considered as weapons of war, David went out to meet Goliath with the calm assurance that God would give him complete success.

Goliath could not believe his eyes. He had to get close enough to get a good look before he would believe the Israelites had sent a mere boy out as their champion. Goliath took David's age and size as a personal insult to his own ability to make war. He probably reasoned that Saul was trying to shame him by sending a scrawny kid to face a giant. Goliath immediately hated David.

*Meanwhile, the Philistine, with his shield bearer in front of him, kept coming closer to David. He looked David over and saw that he was only a boy, ruddy and handsome, and he despised him. He said to David, "Am I a dog, that you come at me with sticks?" And the Philistine cursed David by his gods. "Come here," he said, "and I'll give your flesh to the birds of the air and the beasts of the field!" [1 Samuel 17:41-44]*

Goliath then did what many of us do when we have been shamed. He lashed out. He tried to break through David's calm demeanor by using harsh words. Goliath threatened to present David's body as carrion for the scavengers to feed upon. I am sure Goliath thought he could make easy work of that task. How hard would it be for the giant to overcome a teenager who probably weighed little more than one hundred pounds?

David listened as Goliath spoke. I can imagine David stood firm and confident as he looked up into the face of this enormous warrior. When Goliath finished his tirade it was David's turn to speak and when David spoke, God's truth was revealed.

*David said to the Philistine, "You come against me with sword and spear and javelin, but I come against you in the name of the LORD Almighty, the God of the armies of Israel, whom you have defied. This day the LORD will hand you over to me, and I'll strike you down and cut off your head. Today I will give the carcasses of the Philistine army to the birds of the air and the beasts of the earth, and the whole world will know that there is a God in Israel. All those gathered here will know that it is not by sword or spear that the LORD saves; for the battle is the LORD's, and he will give all of you into our hands."* [1 Samuel 17:45-47]

Confidence in God emboldens us in the face of the enemy.

David went straight to the point. The first order of business was to show Goliath his fate. David enlightened Goliath by demonstrating the inferior status of the warrior's weapons. The power wielded by Goliath's arsenal was minuscule when compared to the power of the weapon David would employ. David would use the name of the LORD Almighty as his weapon. Not one of Goliath's physical attributes, no part of his tactical ability, nothing in his armor and no sword in his hand could stand up against the power found in the name of the LORD.

David continued by sharing with Goliath what would be the outcome of a one-sided fight. Not only would Goliath lose his head, but David further informed him that by the LORD's hand, the Philistine military would enjoy the fate Goliath had earlier promised David. They would become carrion - dead, putrefying flesh. Goliath's comrades would be served up to the birds and the wild beasts for supper. Why would this mass carnage be necessary? So that the whole world would know that there is a God in Israel.

Furthermore, David continued, everyone present would know that God needs nothing and requires no person to accomplish victory. God would save the Israelites and give the Philistines into their hands because the battle belonged to the LORD. God owned it. It was His. God wanted everyone to know who was in control and the Philistines would have the dubious honor of bearing the burden of His desire.

The time arrived for the talking to cease and the action to begin. Very soon the Philistine army would once again make the acquaintance of the God of Israel.

*As the Philistine moved closer to attack him, David ran quickly toward the battle line to meet him. Reaching into his bag and taking out a stone, he slung it and struck the Philistine on the forehead. The stone sank into his forehead, and he fell face down on the ground. So David triumphed over the Philistine with a sling and a stone; without a sword in his hand he struck down the Philistine and killed him.* [1 Samuel 17:48-50]

By his actions David once again confirmed his confidence in God. Not only did David step out to accept the challenge of his enemy, he ran toward him, confident in God's ability to deliver him.

| Confidence placed in God earns His honor. |

God honored David's confidence that day. With a stone and a sling David felled the huge warrior. When Goliath finally hit the ground, he fell face down before the power of God. What more appropriate position for an enemy of the LORD to assume.

*David ran and stood over him. He took hold of the Philistine's sword and drew it from the scabbard. After he killed him, he cut off his head with the sword. When the Philistines saw that their hero was dead, they turned and ran.* [1 Samuel 17:51]

Goliath's death did not end the battle. Remember, Goliath had defied God. God wanted the Philistine's destruction to be complete so there would be no doubt that divine intervention had occurred. With Goliath's own sword, David cut off the giant's head. This action prompted the Philistine army to turn and run.

David had run toward his problem with confidence in God's ability to overcome. When David came face-to-face with the dilemma, God intervened and David conquered the giant. As David stood over the felled warrior, he looked out and saw what was left of his problem, the remainder of the Philistine warriors, turn and run. David's confidence had not been misplaced. God's deliverance was complete.

David became a leader that day. When the Israelite warriors saw how David's confidence in God had been transformed into victory, they were eager to follow his example.

*Then the men of Israel and Judah surged forward with a shout and pursued the Philistines to the entrance of Gath and to the gates of Ekron. Their dead were strewn along the Shaaraim road to Gath and Ekron.* [1 Samuel 18:4]

**Parent to Teenager**: Without confidence in God, you will never reach your full spiritual and emotional capacity. As your parents, we have the responsibility to teach you how to have confidence while avoiding the risk of trust misplaced. In order for you to escape failure, it is imperative that you place your confidence in the One for whom failure is impossible. God expects you to be confident in Him. When you meet this expectation you have the opportunity to develop to your highest potential.

## Rules to follow:
Place your confidence in God, knowing He will never fail.
Stand firm before your enemies in your confidence in God.
Trust God for victory in your life.
View circumstances from God's perspective.

**Father,**
Help me learn to be confident in you. As I learn, help me teach my child. Give me the courage to run toward my problem secure in the knowledge of your ability to overcome that problem through me. Help me be willing to serve as I await my position in your kingdom. May my child see in me an example of a Godly leader.

# Chapter Four

## God Expects Patience
### Joseph

*So when the Midianite merchants came by, his brothers pulled Joseph up out of the cistern and sold him.* [Genesis 37:28a]

Excitement is a state of mind that often enables a person to achieve at a level that would otherwise be impossible. At times excitement is produced from a sense of accomplishment and can invoke feelings of euphoria. At other times, excitement stems from a crisis situation and can leave a person feeling quite helpless. Whether caused by crisis, accomplishment or just the anticipation of either possibility, excitement is an emotional condition worthy of study.

As we become excited, our bodies produce a substance

called adrenaline. The hormone adrenaline stimulates the body mechanisms that help us take emergency action. Science has shown that the ability to perform outside the realm of normal achievement is directly related to the amount of adrenaline found in the bloodstream. The more excited we become, the more adrenaline produced.

Medical personnel have documented reports of persons who have exhibited super human characteristics when excited by a series of catastrophic events. This emotional high has often enabled that person to rescue another from certain death. I have heard news accounts of people realizing a momentary surge of strength that allowed them to lift objects as heavy as a car or a tractor. In every case, the action seemed to go beyond the limits of human ability. Superhuman strength notwithstanding, there are drawbacks to an elevated adrenaline level.

It has been my personal experience that, except in situations of extreme danger, one's ability to reason is inversely proportional to the level of adrenaline being produced. (I am aware my personal experiences cannot replace scientific investigation, but I do believe they may warrant consideration.) It is the notation of this observed relationship that gives substance to my hypothesis: the more excited one becomes, the less prone one is to make calculated, thoughtful judgements. This inverse association of adrenaline level and cerebral function may be the mitigating factor in the process known as "jumping to a conclusion". When this condition occurs, deductive reasoning ceases and patience dissolves in antipathy.

To lend credence to my hypothesis, I would like to present for your consideration data based upon my personal experiences with some very excitable people.

The two groups that have provided unlimited opportunities for observation are mothers and football players.

I realize these two subsets of humans are too different for the consideration of routine data. However, if you will be patient, I will show there does exist a connection which validates my logic in pairing these two groups. (Please note that for the sake of our study, the word *patient* will be defined as "bearing misfortune or pain without complaint".)

Mothers and football players are more similar than most people realize. Both groups contain participants who are hardy, hard-working, and trainable. I have never quite understood, however, a football player's need for so many coaches and trainers since there is no NFL playbook more elaborate than one mother's car pool schedule.

Mothers and football players are also dedicated to their jobs in a manner which goes beyond normal expectations. Who other than a football player would relish the opportunity to be abused by his co-workers; and who but a mother would cheer for him as he took it.

Also, members of each group exhibit a zealous desire to be thought of as friendly. To study this phenomenon firsthand, simply watch what happens when any mother or football player becomes aware of surreptitious observation. Without fail, both will react involuntarily, producing a smile that would melt an iceberg.

Another affinity is the tendency of members in both categories to use the first finger of their right hand as a tool of communication. I need to insert that mothers have outclassed football players in the ability to elicit a response through the use of this tool.

And, finally, specimens in the two groups share a proclivity to exaggerate the significance of any action or event in which they participate.

Let's look first at the group of people we call football players. Do you recall the first time you watched as a football player crossed the goal line? Remember how, after a brief pause, his body began to exhibit a series of disfiguring gyrations that seemed to be connected with the scoring of points? You know what I mean. You have seen it on national television a hundred times. The score is close and the home team has the ball on its own forty yard line. With less than a minute to go in the game, the tight end breaks free and cuts back across the middle. Just as he splits the secondary, the quarterback releases a shot that leads perfectly into his hands. As the ball is tucked safely under his left arm, the tight end breaks a tackle and heads for the end zone. With a well positioned block at the right moment, he glides across the goal line as the thunderous applause of the hometown fans rock the stadium. The touchdown puts the home team ahead. Everything points to a win and the excitement is like an electric current flowing through the crowd. Then, without warning, the tight end bends his knees, slides up on his tiptoes, and with his arms flailing above his head, does a dance with all the elements necessary to produce a thunderstorm in a whirlwind.

I believe it is safe to assume that any player who has scored points for his team will feel some degree of excitement. I also believe it is a natural progression of events that the player should express his excitement in some legitimate manner. I cannot agree, however, that the player would chose this form of self-expression were he using all his cognitive faculties. The football player is solid evidence in favor of my hypothesis. The more excited one becomes and the more caught up one is in one's circumstances, the less likely one is to exhibit rational behavior.

As a mother and a member of the second group in my study, I am able to share personal testimony of an event that lends support to my hypothesis.

The year was 1983. K'Anna was one month away from completing her first grade year at Florence Elementary. Like most social butterflies, K'Anna felt it was her civic responsibility to be involved in every activity that might be school related. I was not surprised, therefore, to see a letter from Mrs. Dianne Roberts describing a jump rope contest to benefit the Heart Association; nor was I surprised to find that K'Anna had already signed up. The day finally arrived for the contest. After two weeks of practice, K'Anna and Dave were the first ones in the car that Saturday morning. As usual, we were ten minutes late leaving home. The tardiness factor had become an integral part of our lives since the birth of our third child. Because the school is about seven miles from our home, I hoped to recover about half of the lost time. As I pulled onto the street, my thoughts were absorbed with a speed versus distance calculation. Little did I realize the harrowing ordeal I was about to experience.

Precisely as calculated, we arrived at the school gym less than ten minutes later. Because Luke was only fifteen months old and had mastered the art of walking just well enough to disappear at a moment's notice, I knew I would need help to keep him in tow during the contest. For this reason, as we were parking, I cautioned Dave and K'Anna to help me keep an eye on Luke.

The car engine had barely stopped when K'Anna and Dave unbuckled and jumped out. Dismissing the rising sense of panic their attempt at a speedy departure caused, I called for the pair to stand by the car until I could get Luke out of his car seat.

Never having had much success at putting grasshoppers in a box, I was not completely surprised when, as I closed the car door, I saw Dave and K'Anna race for the gym. Turning just as the two blond heads meshed with the crowd, I knew the reason for my sense of panic: I had received a premonition of what was to be. Dave and K'Anna were clearly visible, but Luke was not to be found. Only a few seconds had ticked off the clock, but in those few moments, Luke had vanished.

I cannot describe the feeling of hopelessness that welled up inside me as I looked to where K'Anna and Dave were standing. Luke was not with them. The level of excitement I felt at that moment caused my brain to elevate to a gear I had never known existed. My heart began to pump wildly, forcing the adrenaline to speed on its course through my bloodstream.

My ability to form logical, coherent thought disappeared into oblivion. I could not focus. I could not get the situation into perspective. The patience to reason through this crisis had vanished with Luke. Rational thought was not possible.

Even now, as I relate the details of this incident, I maintain a vivid remembrance of my emotional state at that moment in time. Just the consideration of what might have been causes an elevation in my blood pressure and a quickening of my pulse.

With a sense of panic common to cornered animals, I quickly scanned the crowd as I called out to K'Anna and Dave, "Where is Luke? I told you to help watch him and now he is gone!"

The reason for the look of incredulity from Dave and K'Anna did not penetrate my befuddled brain until I heard a sweet little voice at my ear say, "Here me, Luke."

Hearing Luke's voice caused my level of excitement to diminish to the point where I could again use my powers of deductive reasoning. Turning toward that welcomed sound I looked and there on my hip, where he had been the entire time, was Luke patting his chest. I was holding him.

Just as the impact of my actions cleared the haze in my brain, my mother stepped up behind me and whispered, "No matter how much they torture you, never admit to anyone what happened here today!"

I have diligently honored my mother's advice on this matter until today. I believe, however, that the recounting of this event, more than any other, confirms my hypothesis: The more excited we become, the less likely we are to form rational thought.

As our decision making capability turns to mush, so does our ability to put our circumstances into a proper perspective. Without the proper perspective, we lose our propensity for patience. And it is patience, my friend, which God expects from all of us.

> Three definitions of patience are: (1) the bearing of pains or trials calmly or without complaint; (2) the manifesting of forbearance under provocation or strain; and (3) the ability of being steadfast despite opposition, difficulty, or adversity.

## Joseph Exemplifies Patience

Though he had ten older sons, Joseph was clearly Jacob's favorite.

*Now Israel loved Joseph more than any of his other sons, because he had been born to him in his old age; and he made a richly ornamented robe for him.* [Genesis 37:1]

Jacob did nothing to hide his special love for Joseph. Whatever the motives for his actions, Jacob's other sons noticed his preferential treatment and hated their brother because of it. So blinded was Jacob by his love for Joseph that he lavished expensive gifts on him without thinking how his actions might appear to his other sons. He even made the mistake of allowing Joseph to become a tattle-tale, reporting the bad things his brothers did.

By the time Joseph was seventeen, Jacob's partiality for Joseph had worn thin with the other boys. I'm sure Joseph's constant presence among them did nothing to soothe his brothers' rancor. The situation became more and more tense so that, in time, Joseph's brothers could not say a kind word about him.

Just when the pressure on the family seemed to be at the point of explosion, things got worse. The little piece of straw arrived. Yes, it was that same piece of straw that always seems to show up at the worst possible moment. I'm sure it has appeared on your doorstep from time to time. You know the one. That small, dried blade of grass that always manages to break the camel's back.

One night as Joseph slept, God revealed his future. God gave him a dream and like any normal teenager, Joseph felt compelled to share his good news with his brothers. The more Joseph talked about the dream, the more his brothers hated him.

*He said to them, "Listen to this dream I had: We were binding sheaves of grain out in the field when suddenly my sheaf rose and stood upright, while your sheaves gathered around mine and bowed down to it."* [Genesis 37:6-7]

> God gives dreams of His plan for our future, but He expects our patience as His plan unfolds.

If there was ever a textbook case of what *not* to do when you want to win friends and influence people, this was it. It is hard for me to imagine that even a seventeen-year-old would overlook the potential hazards in sharing this type of information with a group of men who clearly despised him. Joseph, however, would not be deterred.

The Scripture is unclear on whether Joseph's boldness held root in his father's protection or if the boy was just not thinking past his nose. Either way, Joseph gave his brothers a glimpse into their own futures that day. Little did any of them know the heartache this family would endure before Joseph's dreams found fulfillment.

Whatever his reason for sharing his dream, this tidbit of information set the flame to a fire that would burn out of his control.

*His brothers said to him, "Do you intend to reign over us? Will you actually rule us?" And they hated him all the more because of his dream and what he had said.* [Genesis 37:8]

The most interesting facet of the brothers' reaction to Joseph's news was the correctness of their interpretation. I have found that often we muddy the waters of God's revelation by trying to make theologically sound deductions rather than just taking God at His Word. Joseph's brothers did not have that problem. They heard the dream as Joseph recounted it, then, without pause, they arrived at a straightforward, no frills, interpretation.

And if one dream was not enough, Joseph had another one.

*Then he had another dream, and he told it to his brothers. "Listen," he said, "I had another dream, and this time the sun and moon and eleven stars were bowing down to me."* [Genesis 37:9]

This time, Joseph shared his dream with his brothers *and* his father. Joseph probably included his father in the news since Jacob was referenced in the dream. I am sure you arrived at the same reasonable interpretation as Joseph's family did over this bit of news.

*When he told his father as well as his brothers, his father rebuked him and said, "What is this dream you had? will your mother and I and your brothers actually come and bow down to the ground before you?" His brothers were jealous of him, but his father kept the matter in mind.* [Genesis 37:10-11]

Let's look at this from Joseph's perspective for a moment. It must have been difficult for this young man not to get excited about this news.

As Jacob's son, Joseph served the God of his father Abraham. Joseph was aware of the significance given dreams and visions which were sent from God.

I can visualize the pumping action of the adrenal as it

spewed its hormone into Joseph's system. Just to imagine, even for a moment, that his father, his mother, and especially all his brothers would bow down to him must have given Joseph a taste of euphoria beyond his wildest imagination. Surely Jacob's cool reaction to Joseph's dream was the only factor keeping the boy's feet on the ground.

So that we do not miss God's perspective in this situation, let's pause here for a moment. God had a plan. This fact was obvious when Joseph had the dream. The plan was to give Joseph a position of responsibility and authority. The position Joseph would one day hold would be so significant that along with Joseph, his brothers, his father, and his mother would learn to meet God's expectation of patience. This lesson was critical for Joseph and his family because through Joseph's patience, God would provide for a nation.

> In the midst of set-backs, God expects us to remain patient as He brings about His plan for our lives.

A short time after the dream episode, Jacob's ten oldest boys were out tending his flocks. Jacob wanted to hear of their progress, so he sent Joseph to find them. When Joseph arrived at the place Jacob had mentioned, his brothers were not there. Joseph inquired of one of the locals and found that his brothers had moved on toward Dothan. Because sheep crop the grass near the root, it was necessary to move the herd from place to place in order to avoid ruining the pasture.

The Scripture gives no hint that Joseph knew of his brothers' resentment for him. If Joseph did know, he seemed unconcerned about their continued anger. As he approached the herds at Dothan, Joseph's brothers saw him and began to make a plan to get rid of him.

*But they saw him in the distance, and before he reached them, they plotted to kill him.* [Genesis 37;18]

What a sad commentary that God's men could become so jealous of one of their brothers they would devise a plan to kill him. This was the state of affairs into which the seventeen-year-old Joseph walked.

*"Here comes that dreamer!" they said to each other. "Come now, let's kill him and throw him into one of these cisterns and say that a ferocious animal devoured him. Then we'll see what comes of his dreams."* [Genesis 37:19-20]

Good men, Godly men, were reduced to liars and schemers all because of jealousy. As the brothers plotted a way to kill Joseph and then cover up their involvement in his death, Reuben, Joseph's oldest brother, realized he could not be a part of their scheme. He wanted to save Joseph from the other brothers and devised his own plan for Joseph's rescue. Reuben's plan was to eventually take Joseph home without any harm done.

*When Reuben heard this, he tried to rescue him from their hands. "Let's not take his life," he said. "Don't shed any blood. Throw him into this cistern here in the desert, but don't lay a hand on him." Reuben said this to rescue him from them and take him back to his father.* [Genesis 37:21-22]

Reuben thought he had the boys convinced. If all went well, he would have Joseph out of the well and back home in no time.

*So when Joseph came to his brothers, they stripped him of his robe -- the richly ornamented robe he was wearing -- and they took him and threw him into the cistern. Now the cistern was empty; there was no water in it.* [Genesis 37;23-24]

How disillusioned Joseph must have felt sitting at the bottom of that well. It had been only a short while ago that he felt invincible. Now the adrenaline running through his body was caused by despair. What good would his dream be to him now? His brothers' hatred for Joseph was so great that he was not likely to ever again see the light of day, let alone have the sun, moon, and stars bow down to him. As Joseph contemplated his circumstances, his brothers were having their evening meal.

*As they sat down to eat their meal, they looked up and saw a caravan of Ishmaelites coming from Gilead. Their camels were loaded with spices, balm, and myrrh, and they were on their way to take them down to Egypt. Judah said to his brothers, "What will we gain if we kill our brother and cover up his blood? Come, let's sell him to the Ishmaelites and not lay our hands on him; after all, he is our brother, our own flesh and blood." His brothers agreed.* [Genesis 37:25-27]

Notice now who is in charge. It is not Reuben. As a matter of fact, Reuben does not even appear to be a part of this conversation. Judah has taken over as the leader of the brothers. Reuben thought he had things under control. Little did he know the turn these events would take.

I am sure the brothers salved their consciences with their exalted sense of family obligation. They could have killed Joseph, but they did not. They actually did Joseph a favor. They sold him into slavery rather than take his life. After all, Joseph was their flesh and blood. This was the least they could do.

How many times do we offer excuses for our own behavior by pointing out how much worse things could have been. "Why, honey, I know I didn't need a new dress, but I found it on sale. If I had bought it before Christmas it would have cost a fortune. I must have saved at least fifty dollars!"

Or how about this one: "Ah, baby. I'm not like most of the guys. Why, during hunting season they don't think twice about missing church every week. I was only out for a couple of Sundays. It wasn't all that bad, was it?"

*So when the Midianite merchants came by, his brothers pulled Joseph out of the cistern and sold him for twenty shekels of silver to the Ishmaelites, who took him to Egypt.* [Genesis 37:28]

When Reuben returned, Joseph was gone. As the oldest brother, Reuben knew his position of responsibility. It did not matter that he had disagreed with his brothers' scheme. It did not matter that he had planned to rescue Joseph. It only mattered that Joseph was gone and someone had to break the news to Jacob.

*When Reuben returned to the cistern and saw that Joseph was not there, he tore his clothes. He went back to his brothers and said, "The boy isn't there! Where can I turn now?" Then they got Joseph's robe, slaughtered a goat and dipped the robe in the blood. They took the ornamented robe back to their father and said, "We found this. Examine it to see whether it is your son's robe."* [Genesis 37:29-32]

These boys just would not give up. They had created a mess and now they were drawing their own father into the web of deceit. I can imagine they reasoned it was better for Jacob to lose one son through a lie, than lose all of his sons through the truth. Once again, we get a vivid picture of the type boys Jacob had raised.

*He recognized it and said, "It is my son's robe! Some ferocious animal has devoured him. Joseph has surely been torn to pieces." Then Jacob tore his clothes, put on sackcloth and mourned for his son many days. All his sons and daughters came to comfort him, but he refused to be comforted. "No," he said, "in mourning will I go down to the grave to my son." So his father wept for him.* [Genesis 37:33-35]

Joseph may have died in Jacob's mind that day, but Joseph's life was far from over. The men who purchased Joseph from his brothers wound up in Egypt where they sold Joseph to Pharaoh's Chief of Security.

*Meanwhile, the Midianites sold Joseph in Egypt to Potiphar, one of Pharaoh's officials, the captain of the guard.* [Genesis 37:36]

Hind sight is twenty-twenty. It is a simple thing for us to examine Joseph's circumstances and then realize God's involvement and provisions. After all, we were not there. We did not have to hunker down in the bottom of that well, contemplating what our brothers planned to do next. We were not required to face the agony of believing we would never see our father again. We did not have to walk behind that stinking camel for all those miles. We did not face days and days without a decent meal or a hot bath. We were not required to come to terms with our own brothers' abhorrence. The only thing we had to do was read the account from the Scripture. Joseph had to live it. Joseph had to trust God's heart when it was impossible to see God's hand. To survive, Joseph had to be patient.

> In the middle of a difficult situation, God still expects us to have patience in waiting on the fulfillment of His plan for our lives.

Through patience, Joseph learned a lesson which eludes some of us for a lifetime: Our circumstances do not affect our position with God. Even though Joseph's circumstances had dramatically changed, taking Joseph from favored son to forgotten slave, Joseph's position with God never wavered. What God had revealed to Joseph in his dreams was still valid. God was in control of Joseph's life just as completely as He had been when Joseph was in Jacob's house.

*The LORD was with Joseph and he prospered, and he lived in the house of his Egyptian master.* [Genesis 39:2]

> In the midst of adversity, we must have patience as God works out the details of His plan for our lives.

Joseph was learning the lesson of patience well. Because Joseph believed God's promise, he knew one day he would have a position of authority. But for the moment, Joseph had to set about the task of excelling even in the face of adversity. Rather than give in to the roller coaster ride of excitement and despair, Joseph kept his life on an even keel by accepting his circumstances as part of God's overall plan. He honored God by making the best of a bad situation. As the Egyptian's servant, he worked diligently and God blessed his efforts.

*When his master saw that the LORD was with him and that the LORD gave him success in everything he did, Joseph found favor in his eyes and became his attendant. Potiphar put him in charge of his household and he entrusted to his care everything he owned. From the time he put him in charge of his household and of all that he owned, the LORD blessed the household of the Egyptian because of Joseph. The blessing of the LORD was on everything Potiphar had, both in the house and in the field.* [Genesis 39:3-5]

Notice that Joseph did not need to relate the details of his dreams to gain Potiphar's attention. He simply had to be patient and work hard. God took care of the details. God blessed Potiphar and everything Potiphar owned because of Joseph, and none of this escaped his master's notice. Potiphar knew his good fortune was the direct result of Joseph's presence in his household and soon promoted him to chief of staff.

Being the astute businessman he was, Potiphar later saw the wisdom of putting Joseph in charge of everything he owned.

*So he left in Joseph's care everything he had; with Joseph in charge, he did not concern himself with anything except the food he ate.* [Genesis 39:6a]

Think for a moment how far Joseph had come since being in the bottom of that well. He had survived his brother's anger. That in itself was remarkable. He had survived the treatment of a slave across rough desert terrain. And now, after being sold for the second time, he had risen to a place of authority and esteem in another man's household. Surely Joseph's patience was about to pay rich dividends. Surely the time for Joseph's rise to power was imminent.

Not! As a matter of fact, Joseph's educational opportunities were just about to begin. God was preparing to give Joseph a lesson in patience he would not soon forget.

*Now Joseph was well-built and handsome, and after a while his master's wife took notice of Joseph and said, "Come to bed with me!"* [Genesis 39:6b-7]

Let's make sure we understand the circumstances surrounding this situation. Joseph was no longer responsible for just the household stuff, but was in charge of everything Potiphar owned. He had complete freedom with the operation of Potiphar's home and properties. With this authority came the responsibility for the welfare of Potiphar and his family. So entrenched was Joseph in Potiphar's business that he had become like a member of the family. Joseph answered to no one except Potiphar. Potiphar trusted Joseph completely.

Joseph was probably in his early twenties when Potiphar's wife tried to seduce him. I am sure he was not unlike any other twenty-five-year-old man in his desire to be noticed by the female gender. Since the Scripture points out Joseph's good looks, he presumably had no problem getting a date. But Joseph had a purpose from which he would not be deterred. He had committed himself to God's mission and knew the outcome God had planned for him. Remember Joseph's dreams? Joseph still had the promise of God's best awaiting him at the end of this path of patience.

*But he refused. "With me in charge," he told her, "my master does not concern himself with anything in the house; everything he owns he has entrusted to my care. No one is greater in this house than I am. My master has withheld nothing from me except you, because you are his wife. How then could I do such a wicked thing and sing against God?"* [Genesis 39:8-9]

> Through patience in waiting for the fulfillment of God's promise, we are able to make the conscious choice to honor God by remaining pure and faithful.

Notice Joseph's maturity when he responds to Potiphar's wife. Joseph did not say, "We really shouldn't do this. We might get caught. What if Potiphar comes home and finds us." Nor did he take advantage of the situation with a slight kiss or touch, thinking to end it before it blazed out of control. The Hebrew text uses words which indicate Joseph emphatically declared his unwillingness to participate. The Scripture clearly states that Joseph refused.

Not only did Joseph refuse the advances of Potiphar's wife, he gave her an explanation which allows us a glimpse into a heart which was true to God. Joseph explained his position in Potiphar's house. He explained all the areas of responsibility, as well as the commitment he felt to Potiphar. He also described Potiphar's trust in his ability to do his job. Then Joseph revealed the ultimate reason he would not succumb to temptation. To do so would be a sin against God.

If we could learn only one truth from Joseph's dilemma, I would want it to be this. Any sin, regardless of its nature, is first and foremost, a sin against God. The choices we face each day must be seen from an eternal perspective. No decision is insignificant. As we begin to comprehend this reality we will gain insight which will change the way we make our decisions.

Remember, there are no values apart from God's values. There is no law grater than God's law. There are no consequences and no penalties with greater import than those associated with violating God's requirements.

Like Joseph, we should always evaluate our possibilities with these truths to guide us. Then, like Joseph, we will find a way to honor God through our choices.

Making the right decision the first time was not enough. Joseph had to continue to choose to honor God by remaining pure and faithful. Then he had to go one step further. He had to refuse even to be around Potiphar's wife. She was relentless, but Joseph was more determined.

*And though she spoke to Joseph day after day, he refused to go to bed with her or even be with her.* [Genesis 39:10]

In spite of this complication, Joseph still had his job to do. As he worked, he did everything possible to avoid a confrontation with Potiphar's wife. Then one day, as he was going about his routine, Joseph found himself in a predicament.

*One day he went into the house to attend to his duties, and none of the household servants was inside. She caught him by his cloak and said, "Come to bed with me!" But he left his cloak in her hand and ran out of the house.* [Genesis 39:11-12]

Potiphar's wife would not give up. She became more

and more aggressive until finally, catching Joseph off guard, she tore at his clothes.

Satan is not easily rebuffed. As we choose to turn away from sin and turn toward God, Satan becomes more and more aggressive in his bid for our attention. When faced with this quandary, we should take our cue from Joseph and run!

Joseph did not wait around for an explanation from Potiphar's wife. He knew what she was up to. He did not pause to consider the consequences of being rude to the boss's wife. Nor did Joseph give a thought to what might be said when he left Potiphar's house without all his clothes. Joseph simply saw this temptation for the evil it was and he ran.

What a lesson for our teenagers. I am always amazed as I listen to young people attempt to justify their presence in a less than desirable place by saying, "I was not doing anything wrong. I was just there."

Well, my friends, if doing something wrong is not what you are interested in, then why do you continue to visit a place where wrong is constantly happening?

Learn a lesson from Joseph and stay as far away from evil as possible; and when the situation warrants it, turn and run. Don't let anything or anyone impede your progress toward God's best.

> Even when we suffer unfairly, we can remain patient as we acknowledge that God is still with us and He is still in control of our lives.

Joseph was completely innocent. He had remained pure and blameless before God. He had not touched Potiphar's wife. But Joseph would still suffer. Potiphar's wife lied about Joseph's activities. She accused him of attempted rape. She kept Joseph's coat as evidence of her story. When Potiphar came home he had Joseph put into jail.

At first glance, Joseph's situation seems unfair. Even

though his character had in no way been impugned, his reputation had been destroyed. Joseph was unjustly accused and would pay the penalty for a deed he had no part in. I am certain each of us can identify with Joseph's predicament. We all have had occasions when we have been wrongly accused. Many of us have probably suffered without cause due to an accusation that had no basis in fact. But do not forget this was nothing more than a change in circumstances for Joseph. God's relationship to him had not changed one iota. Joseph's position with God remained steady. God was still in control of Joseph's life.

*Joseph's master took him and put him in prison, the place where the king's prisoners were confined. But while Joseph was there in the prison, the LORD was with him; he showed him kindness and granted him favor in the eyes of the prison warden.* [Genesis 39:20-21]

> In remaining faithful as we await the fulfillment of His promise, we receive God's blessing for our patience.

Of all the prisons to which Joseph could have been sent, he was put in the house of the captain of the guard. This was the prison for anyone who had offended the king. In today's terms it was a federal country club, probably minimum security, and housed the less serious offenders. God was still in control.

*So the warden put Joseph in charge of all those held in the prison, and he was made responsible for all that was done there. The warden paid no attention to anything under Joseph's care, because the LORD was with Joseph and gave him success in whatever he did.* [Genesis 39:22-23]

Even in prison, God made Joseph a success. Through God's intervention, Joseph made friends with the prison warden. Because God continued to prosper Joseph in all that he did, the warden made Joseph the head trustee. Joseph was so diligent in the execution of his responsibilities the warden never questioned him. God continued to bless Joseph in every way.

After Joseph had been in prison for some time, Pharaoh's baker and cup bearer were sent to the same prison where Joseph was being held. Because of Joseph's position, he made friends with the two officials. One morning, Joseph found both men looking as though they had lost their best friend.

When Joseph questioned their melancholia, the baker and the cup bearer told Joseph they had each had a dream. The two were disheartened because they could find no one to give an interpretation. Hearing this, Joseph explained to his two friends that the interpretation for their dreams did not lie with men, but with God.

*So the chief cupbearer told Joseph his dream. He said to him, "In my dream I saw a vine in front of me, and on the vine were three branches. As soon as it budded, it blossomed, and its clusters ripened into grapes. Pharaoh's cup was in my hand, and I took the grapes, squeezed them into Pharaoh's cup and put the cup in his hand."* [Genesis 40:9-11]

After hearing his dream, Joseph gave the cupbearer the interpretation. The cupbearer would be restored to his former position in three days. Just as he had before, he would fill the king's cup and put it into the king's hand. Knowing the cupbearer would soon be in the king's presence, Joseph asked him to speak to Pharaoh on his behalf. Joseph told the cupbearer how he had been taken captive and sold into slavery. Joseph proclaimed his innocence and asked for help to get out of prison.

When the baker heard the favorable interpretation the cupbearer received, he related his dream. Unfortunately, the interpretation for his dream was not as hopeful.

*"I too had a dream: On my head were three baskets of*

*bread. In the top basket were all kinds of baked goods for Pharaoh, but the birds were eating them out of the basket on my head."* [Genesis 40:16b-17]

Joseph informed the baker of his impending demise. In three days the baker would be hung in a tree for the birds to eat.

Three days later the king gave a feast for all his officials. It was Pharaoh's birthday celebration. Just as Joseph had said, the cupbearer was restored to his position while the baker was hanged for bird food.

Being right got Joseph nowhere, or so it seemed. The cupbearer forgot all about Joseph and his plight. To survive his circumstances, Joseph had to dig deeper into his well of patience. God was not yet ready for Joseph's circumstances to change. Joseph was again reminded that God's mission sometimes takes longer than expected.

It was a full two years later before the final stage of God's plan began to take shape. Being right two years earlier would now pay off for Joseph.

The Pharaoh had two dreams which disturbed him greatly. In the first dream, seven healthy cows were eaten by seven other ugly, gaunt cows. In his second dream, seven healthy heads of grain were growing on a single stalk. Then, seven other heads of thin, parched grain sprouted and swallowed the seven healthy, full heads.

When the Pharaoh awoke, he called for his wise men and magicians to gain an interpretation of his dreams. But none of them could help the Pharaoh. Suddenly, the cupbearer remembered Joseph. He related his story to the king about Joseph's interpretations and how each had come true. Pharaoh immediately sent for Joseph.

*Pharaoh said to Joseph, "I had a dream, and no one can interpret it. But I have heard it said of you that when you hear a dream you can interpret it." "I cannot do it," Joseph replied to*

*Pharaoh, "but God will give Pharaoh the answer he desires."* [Genesis 41:15-16]

> In waiting for God to change our circumstances, we must remain patient.

Even after all the trouble Joseph had been put through, even after spending all that time in prison and even after being forgotten by one of the very men he had helped, Joseph still viewed his circumstances correctly. Joseph knew that he held no power to accomplish anything apart from God. He quickly corrected the king's misinformation and explained that it would be God, not Joseph, who would give the Pharaoh an answer.

Upon hearing the Pharaoh's dream, Joseph gave the king God's meaning. The seven fat cows and the seven good heads of grain represented seven good years in Egypt. For seven years God would give an abundant harvest; but after the seven good years, seven years of famine would come. The famine would be so great that the seven years of plenty would be forgotten. Joseph also explained that the Pharaoh was given the same dream in two different forms because the matter had been firmly settled by God.

Joseph then counseled Pharaoh to find a discerning and wise man and put him in charge of all of Egypt. Under this one man's direction, Joseph recommended the Pharaoh appoint commissioners to collect a portion of the harvest during the seven good years. Joseph explained how this food could then be used to feed the people during the seven years of famine.

Joseph's time had finally arrived. It had been thirteen years since he had been sold into slavery by his brothers. His patience would at last be rewarded. After all the years of waiting, Joseph would be given the opportunity to take the position of responsibility and authority for which God had prepared him. God's plan was coming to fruition. Soon God would bless Joseph so he would be in a position to feed a nation, and more.

> *So Pharaoh asked them, "Can we find anyone like this man, one in whom is the spirit of God?" Then Pharaoh said to Joseph, "Since God has made all this known to you, there is no one so discerning and wise as you. You shall be in charge of my palace, and all my people are to submit to your orders. Only with respect to the throne will I be greater than you."* [Genesis 41:38-40]

---
**In waiting for God's blessing, we, through our patience, give a great testimony to unbelievers.**

---

Notice that because Joseph was willing to be patient, Pharaoh was able to recognize the spirit of God in him. What a testimony for waiting on God. As we seek God's best for ourselves and for our children, remember that God operates on a completely different time table than we. While we mark our lives based upon elapsed time, God is concerned with fulfilled time. Had Joseph not met God's expectation of patience, he might have died at the bottom of that well. Or, he could have remained a prisoner in the king's dungeon, where he would be within reach of his destiny, yet never free to touch it.

But Joseph was patient. Because Joseph met God's expectation of patience, God created a position which had never before existed, then promoted Joseph to that position. Joseph was second in command, answering only to the Pharaoh. He was in charge of the whole land of Egypt with Pharaoh's own signet ring to show his authority.

Each time I read the account of Joseph's life, I am amazed by God's sovereign control. Getting Joseph out of Jacob's hands and down to Egypt was a logistical nightmare to say the least. Then, having Joseph imprisoned, so he would eventually meet the Pharaoh's cupbearer, was a feat only God could accomplish. But more than any other sovereign act, Joseph's promotion inspires me to patience.

Let me explain why this one action causes my desire for patience to increase. Throughout history, governments have been established, demolished, and then established again. Men have risen to power, fallen, and then risen again. The Scripture teaches that each transfer of power is accomplished under God's sovereign authority.

How many times in history, however, has a foreigner held the highest appointed position in a monarchy? How many times in any government? Better yet, how many times has a foreign prisoner been appointed to highest position? You can't think of one, can you?

Well, let me go one better. Joseph was a foreign prisoner who arrived in Egypt as a slave. By being patient and waiting for God's best, Joseph went from foreign slave to prisoner and then to governor. And not only did Joseph hold the highest appointed position in Egypt, he was also an overwhelming success. God never does anything half way!

Joseph learned the lesson of patience well. As a result of his patience, Egypt would survive the seven years of famine. Because the famine was not confined to Egypt, Joseph's patience would also impact the lives of his father and brothers. It would be through this famine that God would bring fulfillment of the dreams that had placed Joseph on this path of patience many years before.

*When Jacob learned that there was grain in Egypt, he said to his sons, "Why do you just keep looking at each other? He continued, "I have heard that there is grain in Egypt. Go down there and buy some for us, so that we may live and not die."* [Genesis 42:1-2]

God is so amazing. More than twenty years had elapsed since Joseph's brothers had sold him into slavery. During that time, Joseph had been falsely accused, imprisoned, released, promoted, married, and subsequently had fathered two sons. Many things had changed, but one thing had not. Even though Joseph's circumstances were dramatically different, his position with God was still holding steady. God's relationship to Joseph remained unchanged. God was now ready to reunite Joseph with his family.

*Then ten of Joseph's brothers went down to buy grain from Egypt. But Jacob did not send Benjamin, Joseph's brother, with the others, because he was afraid that harm might come to him. So Israel's sons were among those who went to buy grain, for the famine was in the land of Canaan also.* [Genesis 42:3-5]

After twenty years, Jacob's sadness over the loss of Joseph was still apparent. Benjamin, Rachel's only other son, stayed with his father while the other boys went to Egypt. Jacob refused to take a chance with Benjamin's life. He would not lose him, too.

Because Joseph was the governor of Egypt, he had final responsibility for the allocation of food to the needy. When Jacob's sons arrived in Egypt, they found Joseph in charge of the grain they were sent to purchase. With hundreds of others, they found a place in line and waited to buy grain.

Stepping up to the front of the grain line, the ten brothers did not recognize their own brother when they spoke to Joseph. Joseph's appearance, no doubt, had changed in twenty-two years. At thirty-nine, Joseph probably looked nothing like the seventeen-year-old boy Jacob's sons remembered.

But Joseph recognized his brothers. As they bowed to the ground before him, he remembered his first dream. When their knees hit the ground, God made Joseph's dream a reality.

Think about the excitement Joseph must have felt at

seeing his brothers. I can believe his adrenal glands immediately began to work overtime. The surge of adrenaline through Joseph's bloodstream was probably sufficient to win a chariot race without a horse. But, remarkably, Joseph did not allow the circumstances to rob his perspective. He remained calm and took advantage of his recently completed twenty-two year lesson in patience. He considered the options and made his decision based on fact rather than emotions.

Joseph questioned his brothers thoroughly. Formulating a plan to get Jacob and Benjamin down to Egypt, he accused his brothers of espionage. After holding them prisoners for three days, he sent all but Simeon back to Canaan. Joseph told his brothers he would release Simeon when they returned with Benjamin as the proof of their honesty and innocence.

Before sending them away, Joseph overheard a discussion the brothers were having.

*They said to one another, "Surely we are being punished because of our brother. We saw how distressed he was when he pleaded with us for his life, but we would not listen; that's why this distress has come upon us." Reuben replied, "Didn't I tell you not to sin against the boy? But you wouldn't listen! Now we must give an accounting for his blood."* [Genesis 42:21-22]

The brothers realized an important truth. No matter how much you may regret your actions, no matter how remorseful you may be about a bad decision, you must still deal with the consequences. Hearing their admission of guilt caused Joseph to cry.

After filling their bags with grain and hiding their payment with the grain, Joseph sent the men on their way. When they arrived home, the brothers gave Jacob an accounting of all the events. They sadly related how the governor would not release Simeon or allow them more food until they returned with Benjamin.

Just as they expected, the news did not please Jacob.

*Their father Jacob said to them, "You have deprived me of my children. Joseph is no more and Simeon is no more, and now you want to take Benjamin. Everything is against me!"* [Genesis 42:36]

Even with Reuben's assurances, Jacob would not allow Benjamin to leave. It was not until the grain was gone that Jacob had a change of heart.

*So the men took the gifts and double the amount of silver, and Benjamin also. They hurried down to Egypt and presented themselves to Joseph.* [Genesis 43:15]

When Joseph saw Benjamin, he had his steward prepare a meal for all the brothers. After arriving at Joseph's house with the steward, the brothers became frightened. Gaining the assurance from Joseph's steward that all was right, they went into the governor's house to prepare for the meal. When Joseph arrived, they presented him with gifts and bowed down before him again.

Joseph inquired about his father's health and was told that Jacob was alive and well. When he asked if the young man with them was their youngest brother Benjamin, Joseph became so emotional he had to leave the room.

Later, after gaining control of his emotions, Joseph continued with his plan. After the meal, he arranged for his silver cup to be placed in Benjamin's bag of grain. Into each of the other bags, he again put each brother's silver and sent them on their way. Before the brothers were out of sight of the city, Joseph sent his steward to accuse them of theft. The search that followed found Joseph's silver cup in Benjamin's bag. The brothers could not believe their eyes. They tried desperately to defend themselves, but the steward would not be convinced.

When they returned with the steward to Joseph's house, Joseph offered to free everyone except Benjamin. He proclaimed himself a reasonable man and held that since the cup had been found in Benjamin's bag, Benjamin should be the only one retained. The others were free to return home. I am not sure if Joseph was merely testing the brothers to discover if their loyalty to Benjamin was greater than their loyalty had been to him, or if he thought that by keeping Benjamin, his dad would follow.

Whatever his reason Joseph's actions prompted the brothers to explain the devastation his own disappearance had caused Jacob. They also related in Jacob's own words what would happen should Benjamin not return.

Hearing their story was more than Joseph could handle. He began weeping uncontrollably as he revealed his identity to his family. Joseph's brothers could not answer because they were so terrified. The brother they believed dead for over twenty-two years now stood before them. More than that, he did not seem to be angry for the pain and suffering they had caused.

*And now, do not be distressed and do not be angry with yourselves for selling me here, because it was to save lives that God sent me ahead of you. For two years now there has been famine in the land, and for the next five years there will not be plowing and reaping. But God sent me ahead of you to preserve for you a remnant on earth and to save your lives by a great deliverance. So then, it was not you who sent me here, but God. He made me father to Pharaoh, LORD of his entire household and ruler of all Egypt.* [Genesis 45:5-8]

---

In waiting for God to bring fulfillment of His promise, we, through our patience, develop the ability to forgive and to experience joy.

In a few short moments, Joseph swept away twenty years of guilt. With a complete understanding of God's purpose, Joseph assured his brothers that God had been in control of all their lives the entire time. Because the famine was so great, Joseph correctly surmised that had God not intervened in such a dramatic manner, his family would not have survived. With this understanding, he associated his life's circumstances with the covenant promise given to Abraham. Joseph's joy became complete through his realization of God's perspective.

Joseph sent his brothers back to Canaan to retrieve Jacob, their wives, and all their children. When they returned to Egypt, Joseph sent them to a fertile pasture area known as Goshen. Jacob and sixty-six of his direct descendants moved to Egypt.

The final results of God's intervention and Joseph's patience was never realized by Joseph. God was in the process of providing a means of redemption for all the people of the earth and Joseph's life was just one stepping stone toward this end. To accomplish His goal, God chose to build a nation from which the Redeemer would come.

Through Joseph's patience God provided a place of safety for the burgeoning group. Through Joseph, God gave his people a place to live, grow, and become the nation he had promised Abraham. Because as a teenager, Joseph was willing to meet God's expectation of patience, a mighty nation would one day leave Egypt. From that nation, over fifteen hundred years later, God's promised Hope would come. God gave His Best to us because Joseph was willing to be patient and wait on God.

**From Parent to Teenager:** God expects patience from you. His plans for you exceed even our plans for you - plans beyond our greatest dreams. You must learn to wait upon the LORD. The alternative to patience is not acceptable. You do not want to live your life at the bottom of the well. Without understanding and accepting God's requirement of patience, you will spend a lifetime rushing in and out of circumstances, never achieving God's goals for your life.

## Rules to follow:

**Take time to trust God.**
**Be patient with yourself, with others, and with your circumstances.**
**Remember that your circumstances have no bearing on your position with God.**
**Never let your current situation inhibit your ability to wait.**
**Be patient and allow God to work His miracles through you.**

Father,

Help me learn to be patient. As I learn, help me teach my child. Give me the insight I need to see my circumstances from your perspective. Never let me forget that my circumstances have no bearing on my position with You. Help me always to trust you even when I cannot understand your purpose. May my child see in me a life filled with Hope because I learned to wait on You.

# Chapter Five
## God Expects Purity
### Daniel

*But Daniel resolved not to defile himself.* [Daniel 1:8a]

We live in the age of information. Nothing - no success, no catastrophe, no achievement, no misfortune, no discovery - can occur anywhere on our planet without some news hound gaining the right to broadcast the event. Our need to know drives one of the largest industries in the world. And yet, we still do not know how to live at peace with our neighbor.

Daily, we are bombarded with news bytes that have value only in the mind of some national news director or hometown editor. Data is continuously thrown before us to be sorted, condensed, assimilated, and filed for future use. Our lives are being reduced, bit by bit, to news segments on the ten o'clock report. Somewhere, something has gone dangerously awry.

Through an almost imperceptible process, we have been duped into believing that information, in and of itself, holds some mystical power. As though drawn to this power, the general public spends millions of dollars every day making use of countless avenues for the receipt and transmission of data. Televisions, computers, satellites, radios -- the list of tools is endless and yet we never seem to get enough. We cannot be sated. We will not be sated, my friends, until we realize that information is not a substitute for knowledge.

Where did we lose sight of the true relationship between information and knowledge? To believe they are one and the same is like expecting to drive that picture of a new car right off the page of the magazine. The picture is simply a representation of what might be.

So, too, is information a representation of what knowledge can be. Information is pieces of data strung together. Not all are necessarily true or all necessarily false. Some bits of information are complete, some are not. Each piece in the string might stand alone and produce one pattern of thought, but when combined with any other piece, will produce a completely opposing thought.

Knowledge, however, is the formulation of information into reasonable truths which may be internalized. Knowledge is the basis on which we build our lives. Ultimately, the only real knowledge is generated by the acceptance of the information supplied by God to man.

The confusion arose when as a society we began to relegate to obscurity the most important facet of any piece of information - the source. Source is a most ordinary word, and yet when linked with information, holds an uncommon significance. No information is any better than the source from which it emanates. Unless the source can be qualified, the information has no worth. Information alone has no value for any of us. It is only as we evaluate the source, and then make a decision about that source's value, that the information even becomes usable to us.

Because we have become a society that dismisses the source of our data while placing all our hope on the information itself, we have negated our only true link to real knowledge - God. Hosea explained the problem that results when he said, "...my people are destroyed from lack of knowledge." [Hosea 4:6]

It is not enough to be informed. To survive, we must know. We need the knowledge that comes from God. There is no suitable substitute. Information does not equate to knowledge and it was through my children that I began to understand this truth.

One of my life's goals has always been that each of my children would excel in school. I grew up enjoying the benefits of excellence in my studies and have always believed a report card to be a perfect gauge by which academic success might be measured. Therefore, when my children began their journey into the classroom, I harbored the hope that they too would find the joy that comes with excellence in education. I knew from personal experience that in meeting this expectation, good grades would be the rule, not the exception. I am saddened to say that unless something changes in the next year or two, I will die not having realized this goal.

Even though I may seem dejected over my unattainable goal, a pity party is not necessary. My children are all bright, healthy, energetic creatures. They are all hard workers and are well liked by their peers. Even though school attendance seems to be merely a function of their social calendar, they each pass from one academic level to the next without pause. If there is a problem, it is this: not one of my children can be convinced that the value of an "A" is enough greater than the value of a "C" to warrant all the extra work. And to tell you the truth, the more I listen to the argument, the more convinced I am they might be right.

It was several years ago when I realized their value system might be on a slightly oblique course. The year was 1984, and school had started the previous Monday. Friday was like every other school day. K'Anna had ridden the bus over to the day care where Dave and Luke were enrolled in four-year-old kindergarten and nursery school, respectively.

As a newly promoted third grader, K'Anna was moving up into the new territory of middle school. She and I had spent some time earlier in the week discussing the subtle differences between requirements for the elementary and middle school students. One of the things K'Anna had been concerned about was the increased work load of third year students. I remember listening to her as she described the possible problems that could arise from a twenty-word spelling list.

Concerned about her apprehension, I questioned K'Anna. "Do you think you will have a problem learning all the words?"

"No," K'Anna immediately replied. "But there is so much more after-school stuff for third graders than for the little kids. I just don't know if I'll have the time to learn all twenty words in one week."

Relieved that my daughter was not questioning her ability to learn, I completely ignored my subtle introduction to what would become her lifetime list of priorities.

I was mulling over new tactics for inspiring my children to academic excellence when I pulled my car into the day care on that Friday afternoon. A new angle of approach was in order since, in previous years, a front end assault had proven useless. My children do not respond well to interrogation and torture.

I had decided that my new approach would be to keep a reminder of my goal before them by inquiring each Friday about their progress during the previous week. This way, I thought, the three would not become suspicious of my motives and my goal would be realized. Looking back, I realize now that for my plan to have been successful, someone else would have needed to care.

I was congratulating myself over the craftiness of my idea when K'Anna got into the car that afternoon. As she was fastening her seat belt, Dave and Luke were escorted to the car. After getting the two boys situated on the back seat, I put my new plan into action.

"So, K'Anna," I began, "Did you make straight "A's" this week?" Never let anyone tell you that an adult can out think any child who wants to spar.

Straight "A's" in what?" K'Anna coyly replied. Fifteen seconds had not yet elapsed and already I was behind in the score. I knew I needed to make up lost ground, but I was not sure what to try next.

Hearing our conversation from the back seat, four-year-old Dave interjected, "Mom, I...."

Not wanting to be distracted from my current target, I said, "Just one minute, Dave. K'Anna and I are in the middle of a discussion.' This response was enough to quiet Dave for a moment or two. As I looked in the rear view mirror, I could see that he was already occupied with something in his book bag.

Trying to negate K'Anna's shrewd use of avoidance, I continued with my direct approach. "In school, K'Anna; did you make straight "A's" in school this week?" I knew my comeback was weak, but at least I was holding my own.

K'Anna seemed unconcerned as she quietly turned to face me. Then, with excitement in her voice, she asked, "Did I tell you I can try out for cheerleader this year?"

Suddenly a weak feeling came over me. I know how a person knee-deep in quicksand must feel. Even though the only part of your anatomy stuck in the quicksand may be your feet, you know eventually you will be completely submerged. The feeling of desperation comes when you accept the reality that alone, you have no hope of survival. I was stuck as firmly as I would have been if standing in the middle of a forty acre plot of quicksand.

Trying for one last grasp at the overhanging limb, I asked, "What do cheerleader tryouts have to do with good grades?'

Without even a pause K'Anna responded, "You need good grades to be a cheerleader. Can I sign up?"

Under different circumstances I might have applauded K'Anna's ability to maneuver the conversation to her advantage. However, it was Friday and I had spent a long week at work trying to elicit information from co-workers who seemed just as determined as K'Anna to withhold what I needed. I was not willing to allow my eight-year-old daughter to test her board room technique on me.

Clearing my throat, I gave K'Anna a sidelong glance with my right eyebrow slightly raised. This is the signal used by my husband and me when we want the errant child to know we are not quite buying into his story.

Before I could answer, Dave piped up again, "Mom, I made...."

"Just a moment, Dave. I'm not finished talking to K'Anna."

Again seeing Dave through the mirror, I watched as he took a paper from his bag and pointed to gain Luke's attention. Luke, of course, was undaunted in his endless quest to ignore the rest of the family. After giving Dave a casual glance, he turned back to stare out his window as the world passed by.

To say that I was slightly confused by the turn of events would have been an understatement. What had begun as a passive mission to gain an informal progress report had turned into a full frontal attack. This was the scenario I had planned to avoid. Somewhere things had gotten out of hand. I was in too deep to turn back, so I continued. "Before we talk about cheerleading, let's get back to my original question. Did you make straight "A's" in school this week?"

As I asked the question, I watched K'Anna carefully to gauge her reaction. A professional card player could not have masked his feelings any better than K'Anna did at that moment.

"Jenny's mom said she could try out." Jenny was K'Anna's best friend at school. Only because as a kid I had lived and died by the tactic K'Anna was now trying to use was I able to cut her off at the pass.

"Jenny must be willing to share information with her mom without this mental struggle I am required to experience!" was my retort. Realizing that I had been very close to shouting my response, I looked toward my daughter and offered a quick smile. For a moment I thought I could see a twinkle in the corner of K'Anna's eyes. Then the mask slid back into place.

"Why, Mom," K'Anna sweetly said, "I thought I had answered your questions. What else did you want to know?"

It was at that moment that Dave pounded the back of my seat.

"Mom, Mom," he called out in a panic. The urgency in his voice caused my warning system to elevate to full readiness.

"What is it, Dave? Is something wrong?" I asked.

"Everything is okay, Mom," Dave said. "I just have something to tell you."

"That's good, Dave. I will be ready to listen in just a moment. I am in the middle of finding out how your sister is doing in school." As I rolled my eyes toward K'Anna, I continued, "And I am desperate to know if she is making straight 'A's."

"Before K'Anna could respond, Dave said, "That's what I wanted to tell you."

Long ago I accepted the fact that I am not a rocket scientist. I do, however, like to believe I am able to put more than two thoughts together in a logical arrangement. For me to accept the information Dave had offered, would also mean I had just struggled for ten minutes trying to gain access to a piece of data that was not even secret. This realization did nothing to boost my confidence as a deep thinker. Incredulous that Dave seemed more informed than I, I turned my attention to the back seat.

"You know how K'Anna is doing in school," I stated in disbelief. Even with the knowledge that I was always last in our family to be informed of anything, I still could not believe that my four-year-old had the upper hand on this bit of information.

"No, Mom," Dave laughed and shook his head over how silly his mother could be at times. "How would I know if K'Anna is making straight "A's"? She won't even tell you! But I know how I am doing in school. I am making straight "A's"."

Like a peacock with a new feather, Dave barreled his chest and broke out in a grin of accomplishment. Seeing that Dave was obviously very pleased about something, Luke, using the slow, exaggerated motion common to all two-year-olds, nodded his head in confirmation.

Relieved over my obvious mistake, I absorbed Dave's news. Even though unsolicited, Dave had offered a piece of information I could finally take pride in. At least one of my three children was going to take this business of academics seriously. Feeding off of Dave's obvious rise in self-esteem, I decided to take this opportunity to divert the attention completely to Dave and his grades. In doing so, I hoped K'Anna would see how important it was to excel at her studies.

"Dave, this is wonderful news. I cannot tell you how proud Mom is to hear that you have made straight "A's." So Dave would be convinced of my sincerity I continued, "Dad will be thrilled to hear what you have done. It is not an easy task to make straight "A's", Dave. Not everyone is able to do it."

Seeing the expression on Dave's face change from exhilaration to bewilderment caused me to ease up on the accolades. I watched as he cocked his head to one side and looked toward K'Anna then over at Luke. I glanced briefly at Luke to see that he continued to offer the world his slow nod of affirmation. Suddenly I realized the cause of Dave's anxiety. After all, I silently reasoned, Dave would not want K'Anna to feel slighted if she could not accomplish the same feat.

Before I could reassure him, however, Dave gave an explanation that forever more would change the way I view all information.

"I always make straight "A's", Mom," Dave replied in a perplexed tone. "I thought you knew. Luke's the one who makes them crooked!"

I never did discover exactly how K'Anna had done that week on her grades. What I learned, however, has been more valuable to me than any set of grades my children could ever hope to produce. I learned that information will never be a suitable substitute for knowledge.

---

Make a list of compromising choices which faced you as a teenager. Make a second list of compromising choices which face your teenager. What resulted when you compromised your convictions? How can you help your teenager make correct choices?

---

## Daniel Chose to Remain Pure

Being a teenager in Jerusalem in 605 BC was not easy. Daniel had the normal problems of any teenager. But just when things started to level out and he had his acne under control, his nation began to fall apart at its political seams. Nebuchadnezzar, the crown prince of Babylon, was on the move and headed straight for Judah.

The news of Nebuchadnezzar's approach was no surprise to Daniel. Even before Josiah's death, Jeremiah had been warning of impending doom. As God's true prophet to the nation of Judah, Jeremiah had proclaimed God's anger to anyone who would listen. Those who had believed the Word of the LORD from Jeremiah were not dismayed when told of Nebuchadnezzar's imminent takeover of Jerusalem.

*"O house of Israel," declares the LORD, I am bringing a distant nation against you -- an ancient and enduring nation, a people whose language you do not know, whose speech you do not understand.* [Jeremiah 5:15]

When Jeremiah had prophesied about a foreign nation taking over Judah, the king and many of the people refused to believe. Now those prophecies were about to come true.

A theme that has threaded its way through each of the previous chapters has been the absolute authority of God. Even when men believed they were in control, God has continued His sovereign action.

Jerusalem in 605 BC was no different. Jehoiakim believed he had control of Judah, even though he served as a puppet for the Egyptian Pharaoh. The people of Judah believed they had control because they were God's chosen people, yet they constantly lived in defiance.

Nebuchadnezzar thought he was in control because he was defeating every enemy he encountered. But the truth in the matter was this: God still had control and He was angry.

When Nebuchadnezzar arrived in Jerusalem, the takeover was complete because God had ordained it would be. The Scripture is clear. Nebuchadnezzar did not *take* anything. Rather, God delivered everything into his hands.

*In the third year of the reign of Jehoiakim king of Judah, Nebuchadnezzar king of Babylon came to Jerusalem and besieged it. And the LORD delivered Jehoiakim king of Judah into his hand, along with some of the articles from the temple of God.* [Daniel 1:1-2a]

As part of the Judean nobility, Daniel had taken advantage of the opportunities he had been afforded. He had studied the Scripture and listened to God's prophet. Daniel and his friends were healthy, well-educated teenagers who had been given every privilege. But above all else, they loved God and wanted to serve Him.

What an alarming turn of events this invasion became for Daniel and his friends. Their lives would never be the same. No more would they study for hours on end with their teachers. No more would they be free to move about the city as they pleased. No more would they worship in Solomon's temple with its wealth of gold and silver surrounding them. Soon they would be carted off to a foreign capital to be brainwashed by their captors.

*Then the king ordered Ashpenaz, chief of his court officials, to bring in some of the Israelites from the royal family and the nobility -- young men without any physical defect, handsome, showing aptitude for every kind of learning, well informed, quick to understand, and qualified to serve in the king's palace. He was to teach them the language and literature of the Babylonians.* [Daniel 1:2-4]

To gain a better understanding of the situation in which Daniel and his friends had found themselves, we will need to play the *"what if"* game. If you have never enjoyed this game, give me a moment to get you acclimated and you will see its value.

Let us assume there is a foreign power capable of taking over our government. After experiencing years of evil leadership in Washington, we wake up one morning to hear on the national news that our country is being invaded. The military muscle at the command of this aggressor is impenetrable. Without so much as one missile fired, a coup d'etat is accomplished at our nation's capital.

As the military regime sets up its power base in Washington, an advance team of educators, scientists, and physical trainers begins a search for the top male teenagers in the country. Their commander has given the team instructions to search out and find those young men who, first and foremost, are physically attractive. To qualify for this draft, the teenagers must be without any physical defect and should be considered handsome. Each should have proof of his academic prowess in all subject areas. Additionally, the young men need to be well-read, up-to-date on current events and fast learners. In general, the team will be searching out the cream of the crop. They want only the best young men our country has to offer because these teenagers will be taken back to the invader's home to serve in the palace of their leader.

Even as you watch the events unfold on national television, you are unable to absorb the ramifications of this search. Along with your children, you stare in disbelief as the cameras relay live footage of teenagers being loaded onto buses headed straight for the airport and deportation.

As the news bulletin is being flashed before the nation, you hear the pounding on your door. Without warning, a search team enters your home and points at your seventeen-year-old son.

After verifying the list of credentials they have in their possession, two team members take your son by his arms and lead him, like a prisoner, from your home.

No amount of crying or screaming will alter their determination to complete this mission. Before you can register a proper protest, your son is gone, pirated off to a foreign land with no hope of escape.

Left with no recourse, you watch as your family is devastated and your homeland and way of life are stomped into oblivion by the foreign aggressor. The only hope you have left for your son is that the Godly training you have given him will be sufficient to sustain him through his ordeal.

Our little *"what if"* game probably outlined the scenario in Jerusalem in 605 BC very closely. Even with Jeremiah's warnings, the nation was unprepared for the takeover. After

Daniel and other qualified teenagers were taken, Judah was left as a Babylonian territory with Jehoiakim installed as the vassal lord. Gone but not forgotten, Daniel and his friends began their lives as servants to a heathen power.

Daniel and the other teenagers were chosen specifically for the purpose of becoming political advisors to Nebuchadnezzar. The kings' plan was to take the young men through an intensive three-year training course to wipe their former way of life from their hearts and minds. It was imperative that they be completely reprogrammed since Nebuchadnezzar knew he would never be any better than his least capable advisor. Their capture would have proven useless if their training was not complete.

Daniel and his friends would be schooled in all aspects of the Babylonian empire. Nebuchadnezzar's goal was to brainwash the teenagers by flooding their minds with information about his people, his country, and his gods. What Nebuchadnezzar did not know, however, was that information is not a suitable substitute for knowledge. Nebuchadnezzar was just a part of God's better plan and it would be God's purposes that would prevail.

Before we move on, let's make a quick comparison of Nebuchadnezzar's goal with what is occurring each day with our own children. As Christian parents, it is our responsibility to raise our children in the nurture and admonition of the LORD. This is a facet of their education that must not be overlooked and cannot be delegated. God expects our obedience on this issue and we will be held accountable. Likewise, the Godly parents of Daniel's day recognized their responsibility for their children's education in righteousness.

Daniel and his friends were kidnapped, and placed in a training program which revolved around the idea that for the Babylonian instruction to be successful, all previous training had to be negated. The indoctrination specifically targeted the religious training of the young men. Nebuchadnezzar knew that

Judah's existence as a nation was based upon the people's belief in the one true God. Nebuchadnezzar also knew that he must demolish the young Hebrews' connection with their nation or they would remain attached to their God. For the young men to be completely committed to Nebuchadnezzar's values, they could not remain faithful to their God.

> **Corrupt influences may tempt us, but Godly training will prevail.**

We, too, live in a nation whose very existence is based upon a belief in the one true God. But each day we send our children to be educated in a system that by law excludes all reference to God's values and by design attempts to negate any Godly training our children may have received. Sounds a little like the Babylonian training, doesn't it? We offer our children classes in the sciences, the arts, history, mathematics, and music while claiming that the God who created our intellect should have no place in our thoughts. Except for the commitment of the Godly teachers in our school system, no reference to God's values would ever be made.

How did we arrive at the premise that Godly training should be separate from our government when the government on which our system of education is based was founded on the truths of the Scripture? More than that, as Christians, why do we continue to elect candidates who promote a system that ignores God? The rationale completely escapes me.

*The king assigned them a daily amount of food and wine from the king's table. They were to be trained for three years, and after that they were to enter the king's service. Among these were some from Judah: Daniel, Hananiah, Mishael and Azariah. The chief official gave them new names: to Daniel, the name Belteshazzar; to Hananiah, Shadrach; to Mishael, Meshach; and to Azariah, Abednego.* [Daniel 1:5-7]

The first part of the young men's Babylonian training changed their eating habits. The young Hebrews' food may seem like a trivial thing to us, but from the perspective of Daniel and his friends, their menu represented a way of life. Meat was a rare dish for an Israelite. More often than not, the meal would consist of vegetables, fruits, cheese, and bread. As a matter of fact, it was bread that eventually became the main focus of the meal. By Jesus' day, bread was so common at each meal that Jesus used the word interchangeably with food.

No longer would God's requirements for food and drink be a consideration when planning the menu. The Judean captives would eat from the king's table. This meant they would have available to them the finest cuisine Babylon had to offer. But the finest cuisine brought with it the very things from which God had protected them. At the king's table they could sample cholesterol, fat, trichinosis laden pork, and other bacteria infused cuts of meat.

The second thing the Babylonian captors did to indoctrinate the young conscriptees was change their names. This might not seem significant until you realize that each of their Hebrew names held a specific reference to God. By changing the teenagers' names, the captors were trying to remove all vestiges of their religious training and their allegiance to the one true God. As a poor substitute, they were given names that referenced the Babylonian deities.

In spite of the integrated attempts by their captors to change the minds and the hearts of the young Hebrews, the training of their parents prevailed. Their Godly instruction held firm. Daniel and his friends remained steadfast in their allegiance to the God of their fathers.

*But Daniel resolved not to defile himself with the royal food and wine, and he asked the chief official for permission not to defile himself this way.* [Daniel 1:8]

Let's recap the progression of events. Daniel was taken out of the environment into which he had been born. He was transported over five hundred miles to a new home and a new way of life. He was offered every opportunity to deny the training of his youth and yet he was able to remain firm in his resolve to serve God. How did Daniel accomplish that feat? How did he turn his back on the temptation that surrounded him?

Daniel made a decision and then stood by it. Daniel purposed in his heart that he would be true to God. Daniel made a decision to remain pure and Daniel's decision would soon open the door to God's knowledge and understanding.

> Society pressures us to be impure, but we can be grounded in our decision to remain true to God.

The next time your teen tries to convince you that the pressure he is under is more than he can bear, please do yourself and your teen a favor. Take the time to explain to your child about Daniel's situation. Make sure you emphasize that Daniel was captured by his enemy and thrown into a position of servitude. He was not able to come and go as he pleased. He was a kid facing a man-sized problem. He was alone in a strange land with no network of support. His family was over five hundred miles away. This was not a vacation for Daniel.

The temptation to give in and fit in was tremendous. If Daniel had decided to ignore God's laws and acquiesce to the desires of his captors, only Daniel would have been the wiser. But Daniel decided against the popular choice. He made the right choice. If *fitting in* meant disobeying God, then Daniel resolved to forever be the square peg in a round hole. Because he was willing to make his choice based on God's desires for him, God intervened on Daniel's behalf.

*Now God had caused the official to show favor and sympathy to Daniel, but the official told Daniel, "I am afraid of my LORD the king, who has assigned your food and drink. Why should he see you looking worse than the other young men your age? The king would then have my head because of you."* [Daniel 1:9-10]

When God intervenes, He goes straight to the source. The person responsible for Daniel was Ashpenaz, Nebuchadnezzar's chief of staff. As the king's official representative, Ashpenaz was a man of authority in the government of Nebuchadnezzar. He was completely committed to Nebuchadnezzar's training program for the young captives and was fully aware that failure could mean his head. Yet, when Daniel asked permission to break training, Ashpenaz agreed.

*Daniel then said to the guard whom the chief official had appointed over Daniel, Hananiah, Mishael and Azariah, "Please test your servants for ten days: Give us nothing but vegetables to eat and water to drink. Then compare our appearance with that of the young men who eat the royal food, and treat your servants in accordance with what you see." So he agreed to this and tested them for ten days. At the end of the ten days they looked healthier and better nourished than any of the young men who ate the royal food.* [Daniel 1:11-15]

> Circumstances are sometimes difficult, but God grants us wisdom to cope with our situation.

Through a friendship Daniel had developed with his captors, God intervened and Daniel was allowed to break the rules that had been established by the king. In doing so, he proved that God's way is the best way.

By making the right choice, Daniel proved that God's formula for purity affected more than just his spiritual well-being. At the end of the test period, Daniel and his friends were also in the best physical condition. Even though God's truths may at times seem to be only for our hearts, His best always affects our entire being.

*So the guard took away their choice food and wine they were to drink and gave them vegetables instead. To these four young men God gave knowledge and understanding and all kinds of literature and learning. And Daniel could understand visions and dreams of all kinds.* [Daniel 1:16-17]

By following God's requirements for purity, Daniel and his friends received knowledge from God. The information had been available all the time, but what God gave Daniel and his friends was the ability to understand the information and apply it to the situation at hand. In addition to knowledge, Daniel received from God the ability to understand dreams and visions.

▼ ▼ ▼ ▶ ▼ ▼ ▼ ◀ ▼ ▼ ▼ ▶ ▼ ▼ ▼

I will never forget the feeling of accomplishment that overwhelmed me when the light bulb in my head switched on for algebra. I had been watching those *x's* and *y's* for days, staring at their parade across the blackboard in Mrs. Parson's classroom.

Every day when the bell rang for fourth period, I would slip into my chair on the third row and wait to see the new methods for management of these unruly little letters. Though I tried, I could not see the value in moving the letters from one side of an equation to the other. Then one day Mrs. Parsons attached a dollar sign to a stray $x$. The second that dollar sign became associated with the symbol of my confusion the $x$ had a source and that source had value to me. From that moment on, I had an understanding of algebraic manipulation. Through understanding, my information was converted to knowledge which I was then able to use for my benefit.

As great as the moment was for me, I must admit that my knowledge and understanding of algebra were not complete.

▼▼▼▶▼▼▼◀▼▼▼▶▼▼▼

What God gave Daniel, however, was complete.

*At the end of the time set by the king to bring them in, the chief official presented them to Nebuchadnezzar. The king talked with them, and he found none equal to Daniel, Hananiah, Mishael and Azariah; so they entered the king's service. In every matter of wisdom and understanding about which the king questioned them, he found them ten times better than all the magicians and enchanters in the whole kingdom.* [Daniel 1:18-20]

When Daniel and his friends were taken before the king, he placed them into service. The king had immediately realized these boys were at the head of their class. But as the teenagers continued to speak, Nebuchadnezzar recognized they were also better than all the other of his present advisors. The Scripture uses the expression *ten times* to describe the magnitude of difference between the youth and their currently installed adult counterparts.

| Purity of character will have a far-reaching impact. |

As a captive teenager, Daniel made the choice to remain pure. He could not have imagined the impact that decision would have on his future. Immediately, Daniel's choice led him to the top of his class. Then as time progressed, Daniel's choice of purity took him to a position of leadership in the king's service.  The time would come when Daniel's choice would be the basis for his reprieve from a death warrant.

A year after Daniel and his friends had arrived in Babylon, King Nebuchadnezzar had a dream.  The dream so disturbed the king that he was unable to sleep.  As the king, Nebuchadnezzar had instant access to the group of his advisors who lived on the palace grounds.  He called this group together.

There were magicians, enchanters, sorcerers, and astrologers, but apparently, Daniel and his friends were not among them.  With his group of counselors surrounding him, the king shared his concern.

*... he said to them, "I have had a dream that troubles me and I want to know what it means."* [Daniel 2:3]

The king's request to have his dream interpreted was not unusual.  What the advisors did not know, however, was that Nebuchadnezzar planned to use his dream as a test for their integrity as wise men.  When the advisors asked the king to relate the details of his dream so they could give him an interpretation, the king's council received the shock of their lives.

*The king replied to the astrologers, "This is what I have firmly decided: If you do not tell me what my dream was and interpret it, I will have you cut into pieces and your houses turned into piles of rubble.  But if you tell me the dream and explain it, you will receive from me gifts and rewards and great honor.  So tell me the dream and interpret it for me."* [Daniel 2:5-6]

What a predicament!  The wisest men in the nation found themselves backed into a corner with no way out.  Let me assure you they had no false hope of being able to relate the king's dream.  If these men knew nothing else, they knew their limits. So they used the tactic we often use when we need to stall for time. They repeated themselves. The level of their anxiety must have been at an all-time high because they made no attempt to cover up what they were doing.

Their tactic was so transparent, the king identified their actions without pause.

*Then the king answered, "I am certain that you are trying to gain time, because you realize that this is what I have firmly decided: If you do not tell me the dream, there is just one penalty for you. You have conspired to tell me misleading and wicked things, hoping the situation will change. So then, tell me the dream, and I will know that you can interpret it for me."* [Daniel 2:8-9]

Given a moment to think, the council took the only available route. They told the king what they believed to be the truth.

*The astrologers answered the king, "There is not a man on earth who can do what the king asks! No king, however great and mighty, has ever asked such a thing of any magician or enchanter or astrologer. What the king asks is too difficult. No one can reveal it to the king except the gods, and they do not live among men."* [Daniel 2:10-12]

Let's take a brief look at the reaction of the advisors to the king's demands. First they told the king what he asked was an impossible task. From the council's point of view, the king had made an unreasonable request. There was not a man alive who would be able to do what the king wanted.

Then they impugned the king's character for having a requirement they could not meet. These boys must have had a death wish. It is one thing to admit your inability to accomplish a task, but to imply that your superior is foolish for even asking is carrying things a bit too far.

Be that as it may, the wise men did not stop there. They further explained that what the king wanted done was just too difficult. The implication was that even if there was one qualified to accomplish this feat, the king should have considered the degree of difficulty as cause to withhold his request.

Finally, they hit upon the real truth. What the king was asking was outside the realm of human possibility. This task would require supernatural intervention. To admit their gods incapable of this deed would be an admission of their own fallibility. Rather than take that path, the wise men dismissed divine intervention as inaccessible.

Before you are too quick to condemn these men, let me ask you a question.

Has *your* King ever asked you to do something which seemed impossible? How did you respond?

Did you begin by saying, "This is too difficult"? Did you continue with, "I'm just one person. Nobody could be expected to tackle this job." Or worse yet, did you try to shame your King into withdrawing His request?

Nebuchadnezzar's council claimed to be the wisest men in the entire Babylonian territory. All the king was trying to do was give them an opportunity to prove it. By relating the king's dream, the magicians and sorcerers could prove their own validity. Their king would then know they were truly wise.

God often asks us to accomplish the impossible as a test of our integrity. When offered the opportunity, can we prove we are really what we say we are? When we say we are trusting God, are we telling the truth? Or, by our reaction to God's request, do we reveal that our trust lies in our own abilities? The next time God gives you a job that seems outside your realm of expertise, maybe it is not your capability that interests God. Maybe He just wants to gauge your ability to recognize your need for Him.

*This made the king so angry and furious that he ordered the execution of all the wise men of Babylon. So the decree was issued to put the wise men to death, and men were sent to look for Daniel and his friends to put them to death.* [Daniel 2:12-13]

## Our purity sets us apart from the group.

Once again, God's man was in the right place at the right time and was still accused of wrongdoing. Daniel had not even been present when the astrologers and magicians had given the king the fateful news. Yet it would be Daniel who would be blamed.

But when the king's officer came to arrest Daniel, Daniel was able to get a reprieve from the king until he could do what the king asked. What Daniel did next is a testimony to the importance of having a prayer partner.

*Then Daniel returned to his house and explained the matter to his friends Hananiah, Mishael and Azariah. He urged them to plead for mercy from the God of heaven concerning this mystery, so that he and his friends might not be executed with the rest of the wise men of Babylon.* [Daniel 2:17-18]

Daniel's prayer partners prayed with him through the night. Because of their faithfulness, God heard and answered their prayer.

*During the night the mystery was revealed to Daniel in a vision. Then Daniel praised the God of heaven and said, "Praise be to the name of God for ever and ever; wisdom and power are his. He changes times and seasons; he sets up kings and deposes them. He gives wisdom to the wise and knowledge to the discerning. He reveals deep and hidden things; he knows what lies in darkness, and light wells with him. I thank and praise you, O God of my fathers: You have given me wisdom and power, you have made known to me what we asked of you, you have made known to us the dream of the king."* [Daniel 2:19:23]

> God gives the wisdom, knowledge, or understanding to accomplish a task and He is to be praised.

Let's pause here long enough to see a truth through Daniel's eyes. Through no fault of his own, Daniel was facing certain death at the hands of his captor. Knowing the power of his God, Daniel sought and received the knowledge needed to save his own life and the lives of his friends.

But when the mystery of the king's dream was revealed to Daniel, he did nothing before he had properly thanked God for the revelation.

Learn this lesson well. Always take time to give credit where credit is due. When God gives you the wisdom, knowledge, or understanding to accomplish the task at hand, do nothing before you have given proper thanks to God.

*The king asked Daniel (also called Belteshazzar), "Are you able to tell me what I saw in my dream and interpret it?" Daniel replied, "No wise man, enchanter, magician or diviner can explain to the king the mystery he has asked about, but there is a God in heaven who reveals mysteries."* [Daniel 2:26-28a]

Daniel never quits. He marches right in to the king who is prepared to behead him and his friends on the spot, and the first thing out of Daniel's mouth is an admission that no man can do what the king has asked.

But Daniel does not stop there. He continues by using the opportunity to share his faith in the one true God. As Daniel reveals the king's dream and the interpretation, Nebuchadnezzar is introduced to the one true God.

*Then King Nebuchadnezzar fell prostrate before Daniel*

*and paid him honor and ordered that an offering and incense be presented to him. The king said to Daniel, "Surely your God is the God of gods and the LORD of kings and a revealer of mysteries, for you were able to reveal this mystery."* [Daniel 2:46-46]

    Because Daniel made a choice as a teenager to remain pure, a heathen king recognized his God as the one true God. As a result of his choice of purity, Daniel was elevated to the position of provincial ruler and was awarded expensive gifts by the king. And because he remained true to God's expectations for him, Daniel requested and received appointments as administrators for his three friends.

**From Parent to Teenager:** God has an expectation of purity from you. As you meet this expectation, God will grant you the knowledge and understanding necessary to give good, Godly advice. Through purity, you will prepare yourself to receive God's revelation. Through purity, you will become an example of God's best.

## Rules to follow:
**Live consistently in every situation.**

**Remember that a given situation should not alter or dictate your choice of behavior.**

**Choose purity in all things so that you will be wise in the ways of God.**

**Praise God as the giver of purity - and of all wisdom, knowledge, and understanding.**

Father,
    Help me to choose purity in all things. As I learn, help me to teach my child. Give me the strength to remain firm even in the face of adversity. Help me to seek your wisdom, your knowledge, and your understanding. As I teach my child, help me to remember that information alone cannot replace a Word from you. In all things, Father, may I give thanks.

# Chapter Six

## God Expects Devotion
### Solomon

*And you, my son Solomon, acknowledge the God of your father, and serve him with wholehearted devotion ...* [1 Chronicles 28:9a]

As I look back over the last forty-three years of my existence, I realize that my time has been divided into segments which are clearly marked by moments of importance. These demarcations are those events I classify as milestones in my life. We all have these moments in time that help us separate into categories the events that give our lives meaning.

For some, a milestone is achieved at that moment a high school diploma changes hands. This simple action seems to announce to the world one's right of passage into adulthood. For others, a quiet *I do* spoken before a throng of teary-eyed witnesses becomes the experience against which all others are stacked. For still others, it is the attainment of a specific financial goal or the birth of a child. Whatever the description, we all have milestones that lend continuity to our existence.

There have been two milestones in my life that stand out more than any of the others. The first was the day of K'Anna's birth. At that instant, Tommy and I went from a couple to a family. Surrounded by no less than forty family members and friends, K'Anna entered the world secure in her station. As the first grandchild on both sides of the family, she would forever more hold a special place in our hearts. That tiny, delicate creature seemed to sense the love we all felt. As I cuddled her, I knew that somehow her birth would become a point of significance. K'Anna's entry into the world would be a moment against which all future events would be marked.

The second milestone was the day K'Anna left for college. Praise the LORD, she was gone! Maybe our lives could regain some semblance of normalcy. For eighteen years our family had been the target of K'Anna's terror. Dave and Luke had suffered the most. As though driven by some innate sense of responsibility, she had made it her business to mastermind her brothers' demise. With profound dedication she continued at her task until the day she left.

Now that she had left, we could sense a glimmer of hope. With any luck, our two sons would recover from the impact of spending their formative years under K'Anna's tutelage. With therapy, the two would reach adulthood with only minimal scarring. So that you do not suppose I exaggerate K'Anna's impact on our lives, let me relate to you one of the many episodes which help form my opinion.

K'Anna took her driver's exam and received her license soon after Tommy had changed jobs. Because his new job required travel, the children and I were often left to our own devices while Dad worked out of town. Initially concerned about his absence, I was somewhat relieved when K'Anna stepped up to take a more mature role in the family. She offered to shuttle the boys to and from their activities. For those of you with a large family, you know how critical the issue of transportation can be.

Soon, K'Anna's role became routine. Each week she arranged and handled the boy's schedules. Trips to the dentist, the orthodontist, and baseball and football practice were all handled without my input. K'Anna even took care of the boys on Wednesday evenings after prayer service. While I stayed for choir practice, she would take Dave and Luke home to finish their assignments and get ready for bed.

Monotony is a strong sedative. Operating under the false sense of security a routine can produce, I was caught completely unaware one Wednesday evening in 1991. The day had begun like every other day. The children left for school and I went to work. Work and school were uneventful and we all met at home around 5:00 p.m. As I had done every other Wednesday, I reminded the boys they would ride home with K'Anna as soon as prayer service was over.

Choir practice went slightly longer than usual that night, but I knew of no reason to be concerned. Dave and Luke were at home under K'Anna's watchful eye. By the time I pulled in the driveway, I calculated they might even have had their baths and gone to bed.

When I unlocked the front door I knew something was wrong. As I stepped into the foyer, K'Anna and Luke greeted me. Dave was conspicuously absent. Brother and sister were standing at ease with their hands behind their backs. My maternal antennae activated immediately. The expression on K'Anna's face looked enough like remorse to make my heart rate increase. As though in contradiction, Luke's eyes were wide and his countenance was laced with excitement. Thinking back, Luke looked as though he were going to burst at the seams. K'Anna remained calm and collected. As strange as it may seem, the impression of these two opposing emotional states calmed me for a moment.

That moment was fleeting. It ended when K'Anna opened her mouth. "Mom, I think I broke Dave's arm." K'Anna's matter-of-fact tone did nothing to allay my fear.

"What?!" Though the only response I could force from my brain was one syllable, that one word completely conveyed my shock to my oldest and youngest children!

Instinct made me want to break and run. I needed to find Dave. In my mind I could see my oldest son with one arm snapped at the elbow, his hand resting on his shoulder - from behind - and his little body racked with pain.

The terror I felt must have shown in my eyes because before I could move, K'Anna spoke again.

"Now, Mom. You need to calm down. It's not as bad as it sounds."

"Just tell me if Dave is all right," I said as I labored to get my panic under control. "I need to hear you say that Dave is okay."

Luke raised his hand to interrupt. I am not certain if his action was triggered by my anxiety or just by his need to say something. However, his raised hand gained our silence, and Luke took charge of the conversation.

"Aw, Mom," he drawled. "You know Dave. K'Anna's never hurt him really bad, no matter how hard she tried."

Those few words from Luke spoke volumes. When I looked back at K'Anna, she was rolling her eyes. Luke was the last person she wanted in on this conversation. For a moment, K'Anna appeared as though she thought the wrong brother had the broken arm.

"Luke!" K'Anna said as she popped him soundly on the back. "You make it sound like I was trying to hurt Dave." Turning back toward me K'Anna continued, "Mom knows I would never hurt Dave on purpose."

The banter only lasted a moment before I was able to

bring their attention back to the problem at hand. Forcing a calm in my voice that I did not feel, I decided to confront the pair head on.

"Where is Dave?"

"He's in his room, Mom."

Sensing I was just before bolting, K'Anna took a step sideways to block my path. Wanting to finish this unpleasantness, she said, "Before you go back there, at least let me tell you what happened."

As K'Anna talked, I could tell she was not overly concerned about Dave's arm. She seemed more troubled by my reaction to her news than by any injury her brother might have suffered.

Wanting to give her the benefit of the doubt, I folded my arms, leaned back against the door jam and said, "Okay, K'Anna. Let's hear it. Explain what happened here tonight."

The silence in the house was deafening. Neither Luke nor K'Anna took their eyes off me.

After a moment's pause, I added, "And K'Anna, just the truth will suffice. No embellishment, please."

After a deep breath, she began. "Okay, Mom, it all happened like this."

K'Anna began her tale by reminding me how important it is for children to be physically fit. "You know how I have been teaching Dave and Luke some gymnastic moves, Mom?"

I nodded an affirmative response. K'Anna had been taking gymnastics since second grade. Her small size belied her strength and her ability in her sport was really quite remarkable. Even though she had not competed in over a year, she remained in excellent shape.

From time to time K'Anna would try to teach Dave and Luke a few simple tumbling moves. I had watched several times as the three had practiced in our front yard. K'Anna seemed very careful to impress on the boys the correct moves and maneuvers.

Suddenly I realized K'Anna had continued to speak. "Well, Mom, we tried a new move tonight and David did not quite catch on."

She paused long enough to let that tidbit of information break through the haze around my brain.

"It all started as I was trying to help Dave and Luke get the feel of a spring floor."

Unless you are familiar with gymnastic equipment, you will not appreciate the effect K'Anna was trying to produce. In gymnastics, the floor exercise is accomplished on what appears to be a large rug covering a wood floor. It is more than a piece of short pile carpet, however. The floor beneath the carpet is designed to give when the slightest pressure is exerted. The resultant counter-force produces a spring effect as the floor rebounds from the impact. Consequently, when a gymnast jumps, the floor catapults the athlete with a force equal to the jump. Words cannot describe the mental picture I drew as K'Anna continued.

"I was lying on my back with my head aimed toward that wall." As she talked, K'Anna walked into our living room and pointed at the west wall. This was a room usually reserved for special company. About twenty-five feet in length, it held our grand piano on one end and a sofa and chairs at the other. As I entered the room, I noticed tables and smaller chairs had been arranged to create a clear lane the full length of the room. The only hindrances were the sofa at one end and the piano at the other.

"Luke went first. I pulled my knees up to my chest and Luke sat on my feet, like this." K'Anna positioned herself on the floor to offer clarification.

When Luke moved to sit on her feet, I stopped him and said to K'Anna, "Just get on with the story."

"Dave gave the count down, I pushed, and Luke flew," K'Anna explained with a shrug of her shoulders.

"It was great, Mom!" Luke said. "I couldn't wait to get

another turn!"

By this time I was beginning to get the picture. Somehow Dave's ride had not been as successful as Luke's. I gained immediate comfort in the realization that K'Anna had not intentionally injured her brother. As the mother of these three miscreants, I welcomed any consolation, however small it might be. The relief must have shown on my face.

Thinking their reprieve was in place, Luke unbridled his obvious excitement. "Wait! Wait! Let me tell what happened to Dave! What a story! It was great!"

The warning in K'Anna's eyes was not enough to get Luke back under control. Before she could stop him, he had begun to tell his version of the event with such exuberance, I thought perhaps he would be willing to sacrifice his brother's other arm to see it all again.

"It was great! Dave got in position on K'Anna's feet. But just as she started to push, he shifted his weight." Luke's careful attempt to put part of the responsibility on Dave did not escape me.

"Before he was ready, K'Anna sent him flying!" Luke jumped up at this point in an effort to imitate Dave's take-off. As he continued, the pitch of his voice rose with excitement.

"He started off shaky, but he recovered immediately."

Barely stopping for air, Luke hurried through his explanation.

"What he lacked in form, he made up for in speed! Dave almost touched the ceiling, Mom! Can you believe it? You should have seen the look in his eyes!"

The more Luke talked and the more animated he became, the more I realized how impressed he had been with Dave's performance.

"Then, just as he began his descent, he saw the piano. He knew that piano was getting a little too close." To emphasize the magnitude of Dave's narrow escape, Luke held his thumb and forefinger on his left hand so they barely touched. With that hand close to his cheek, he squinted his right eye for effect. I got the picture.

"When he saw the piano, he did the only thing he could do, Mom." K'Anna and I both stood with our mouths gaping as Luke continued. I was aghast because of Luke's enjoyment in the recounting of the event and K'Anna was because Luke was being so careless with his information. She knew Luke was cooking her goose and there was not one thing she could do to prevent it.

Mistaking my inability to form coherent sound as his encouragement to continue, Luke said, "He made a mid-air adjustment! Great move! Huh, Mom!"

I just stared at my nine-year-old.

Sounding almost disappointed, Luke continued, "Dave missed the piano at the last moment. That's when I knew he was in trouble."

"Oh," I replied, "And just what made you think Dave could possibly be in trouble?" Luke completely overlooked the sarcasm in my voice.

"The adjustment was going to mess up his landing, Mom. I knew Dave would miss the piano, but that landing was going to be tricky."

"Tricky! Exactly what do you mean by tricky, Luke?"

As though offering a simple statement of fact, with palms up, Luke shrugged his shoulders and said, "He over rotated."

"Well, that clears everything up for me, Luke." I had to fight the urge to throw my hands up in resignation.

Undaunted, Luke continued. "He had to catch himself somehow, Mom. It could have been a lot worse. If he hadn't stuck his arm out to break his fall, he might have really been hurt. I'm tell you, Mom, it was great!

I just shook my head. Remembering Dave, I left K'Anna and Luke in the living room. As I hurried back to his bedroom, reality struck me. K'Anna's devotion to her brothers' destruction was so complete, she had successfully convinced these two to participate in their own demise! To make matters worse, my sons were enjoying the process!

Dave's arm was broken, but his spirit was not! The moment I walked into his room, I saw in his eyes the same glint of excitement I had seen in Luke's. The gleam was only slightly dulled by the pain that accompanies a fracture.

To K'Anna and Luke's credit, they had seen to their brother's comfort. He was sitting up in bed, propped up against a mound of pillows and resting comfortably. With a soft drink within reach, all his needs seemed to be cared for. As I examined his left forearm, I found the telltale swelling that accompanies a stress fracture. Thinking it was my duty as his mother to see to his well-being, I began to get everything lined up for a trip to the emergency room when Dave said, "Mom, did Luke tell you how great it was?"

I know when I'm licked. As Dave began his version of the accident, K'Anna and Luke arrived to provide the necessary animation. I sat silently as the trio recounted in detail the event resulting in Dave's broken arm. As I listened, my thinking changed.

I had been right about only one thing. My three children were devoted. But not in the way I had thought. These three were devoted to enjoying life. They were profoundly dedicated to living the moment at hand. But more than that, they were devoted to each another. They each delighted in the others' presence. They were committed to their relationship. And though there continued to be narrow escapes and poor judgment, their delight in each other has never waned.

Later, after the X-rays and the cast, I remember thinking back over the evening's events. I smiled to myself as I thought about the joy each child gave to the other two. After considering the fun they always had together, regardless of the circumstances, I began to understand a very important truth. Their devotion to each other was the basis for their delight.

As I pondered the relationship between devotion and delight, I began to size up my relationship with God. Suddenly I knew the truth. Somewhere I was missing the connection between devotion and delight. I knew God's commands and His promises well. *Serve Him with wholehearted devotion* and *delight yourself in the LORD and He will give you the desires of your heart.* But until that moment I had not understood the impact my devotion to God could have on my ability to delight myself in the LORD. To fully enjoy a relationship with the LORD and for that relationship to be everything God intended, I had to make a choice. I needed to give God top priority in my life. I needed to be devoted.

> Our devotion to God will pay dividends in the lives of our children.

## Solomon Devotedly Served God

Solomon was the teenager who had it all. More so than any American youth, Solomon had been born with the proverbial *silver spoon* in his mouth. Solomon's family had more money than he could count. He wore nothing but designer clothes, lived in a palatial home, and enjoyed princely status in the community. He was King David's son.

Solomon was different from other youth, but being the son of a king was not what made him different. Solomon was different because he had an advantage that set him apart both then and now. This advantage had nothing to do with any material wealth. Neither did it rely on his personal appeal or abilities. The one thing Solomon had which gave him a marked advantage was a father whose heart was devoted to God.

Warrior king is an accurate description of David's life as ruler of Israel. Under his leadership, God's people became the predominant military force in the world. He fought and conquered all the nations surrounding Israel. Goliath had only been the beginning for David. The Philistines, the Moabites, the Hittites, the Edomites, the Arameans, the Ammonites -- all these and more fell before the sword of David.

*The Lord gave David victory everywhere he went.* [1 Chronicles 18:13b]

Under God's guidance, David built Israel into a great nation.

*And David knew that the LORD had established him as king over Israel and that his kingdom had been highly exalted for the sake of his people Israel.* [1 Chronicles 14:2]

Yes, David was devoted to God. But David was not perfect. As a matter of fact, King David made more than his share of mistakes. Arranging Uriah's death so he could marry Bathsheba was probably the most noted. As with all others, God dealt swiftly and surely with David over that sin. Though David pleaded with God to spare their child, he and Bathsheba watched helplessly as their firstborn succumbed to God's judgment. The life of their baby may have seemed like a high price to pay, but David and Bathsheba both knew David's sin against God was great. Even at his darkest hour, however, David remained steadfast in his devotion to God.

In spite of his sin, David's devotion to God continued to turn his heart back home. Each time he was confronted with his sin, repentance led to God's forgiveness because, for David, repentance was more than just an empty promise. David agreed with God about his sin. David wanted to change. Each time David turned away from his sin and turned toward God, God changed David's heart and his mind about his sin.

As the nation of Israel grew and prospered, so did David's commitment. With each passing year his devotion to God gained new strength. Eventually, David's dedication gave birth to his desire to build a house for God. It was after he had moved into his palace at Bethlehem that he spoke of his desire to Nathan.

*After David was settled in his palace, he said to Nathan the prophet, "Here I am, living in a palace of cedar, while the ark of the covenant of the LORD is under a tent."* [1 Chronicles 17:1]

> True devotion leads to surrendering one's will in acceptance of God's will.

David wanted to build God's temple, but God had other ideas.

*When your days are over and you go to be with your fathers, I will raise up your offspring to succeed you, one of your own sons and I will establish his kingdom. He is the one who will build a house for me, and I will establish his throne forever.* [1 Chronicles 17;11-12]

Even though God loved David, He would not allow David to build his temple. David was a warrior. His job had been to reclaim the land God had given in promise to Abraham. As the greatest military strength in his day, he had accomplished God's desire. But the temple was not part of God's plan for David. The building of God's house was to be reserved for someone else.

*But you will have a son who will be a man of peace and rest, and I will give him rest from all his enemies on every side. His name will be Solomon, and I will grant Israel peace and quiet during his reign. He is the one who will build a house for my Name. He will be my son, and I will be his father. And I will establish the throne of his kingdom over Israel forever.* [1

Chronicles 22:9-10]

Because of his profound dedication to God's sovereign will, David relinquished his greatest dream in favor of God's greater purpose. Once again, he chose to agree with God and allow God to change his heart and his mind. As a result of true devotion, David was able to accept God's desires and make them his own. Solomon, not David, would build the abiding place for God's Holy Spirit.

Even though God would not allow David to build His temple, He did give David the plans and specifications for the magnificent structure. In intricate detail to David, God laid out the materials, the dimensions, and the decorations for His dwelling place. God even outlined the services and ceremonies that would take place in the Temple.

*David said, "My son Solomon is young and inexperienced, and the house to be built for the LORD should be of great magnificence and fame and splendor in the sight of all nations. Therefore I will make preparations for it." So David made extensive preparations before his death.* [1 Chronicles 22:5]

Though David was not allowed to actually build the structure, God did allow him to participate. He set up training programs for the priests and their helpers. He commissioned the forming of the gold and silver finery that would be used in temple ceremonies. Through David the workmen were conscripted to cut the stone for the building. He amassed a great stockpile of materials that would be used in the construction. But not one stone was laid atop another under David's direction. God had spoken. David would not do the work. It would be Solomon, David's teenage son, who would build God's temple.

*Then he called for his son Solomon and charged him to*

*build a house for the LORD, the God of Israel.* [1 Chronicles 22:6]

With all his preparations for the temple completed, David knew his death was fast approaching. Before he could leave, however, he had one last task to complete. The nation must know God's choice for his successor. In his final act as Israel's warrior king, David transferred leadership of the Nation of Israel to his son Solomon. His actions left no doubt in the people's hearts that Solomon was God's choice.

*Of all my sons -- and the LORD has given me many -- he has chosen my son Solomon to sit on the throne of the kingdom of the LORD over Israel. He said to me: 'Solomon your son is the one who will build my house and my courts, for I have chosen him to be my son, and I will be his father. I will establish his kingdom forever if he is unswerving in carrying out my commands and laws, as is being done at this time.'* [1 Chronicles 28:5-7]

| Devotion to God leads to favor with God. |
|---|

As the king, David gave Solomon a great gift that day. A nation united, God's nation, was handed to Solomon to rule. Wealth and promise beyond measure were meted out to David's teenager on that fateful day. But David's greatest gift to his son was not the crown or the wealth that accompanied it. With the transfer of power, David gave to Solomon something of much greater importance than the throne of a nation. Solomon received from his father the gift God wants each of us to give our children. David gave Solomon the example of a heart profoundly dedicated to God.

Though encumbered with a lifetime of sin, David had made knowing God his top priority. After each encounter with God, David was changed. Gradually, his desires gave way to

God's purposes. The more David changed, the more he reflected God's heart. David's life of devotion eventually became his true legacy.

As much as David desired to build God's temple, he desired even more that Solomon would be devoted to God. He knew that God would first need to rule in Solomon's heart before Solomon could rule God's people. So David gave his teenager a piece of advice laced with the wisdom of a man after God's own heart.

*"And you, my son Solomon, acknowledge the God of your father, and serve him with wholehearted devotion and with a willing mind, for the LORD searches every heart and understands every motive behind the thoughts. If you seek him, he will be found by you; but if you forsake him, he will reject you forever. Consider now, for the LORD has chosen you to build a temple as a sanctuary. Be strong and do the work."* [1 Chronicles 28:9-10]

Excellent advice for a king, don't you think? What about for a teenager? What about your teenager?

David's advice was not lost on Solomon. Solomon would build the temple in accordance with the plans and specifications handed him by his father. Solomon would take the material David had collected and transform it into a beautiful place for the indwelling of the Holy spirit of God.

Before he would build the temple, however, Solomon knew he must humble himself before God. Solomon understood that God must have first place in his heart. He desired to acknowledge the God of his father and serve Him with wholehearted devotion.

After David's death, Solomon gathered the whole assembly of Israel and went to the high place at Gibeon. In accordance with the Law given to Moses, Solomon offered burnt offerings to the LORD. Like his father David, he loved the

LORD and understood God's expectation of devotion.

*That night God appeared to Solomon and said to him, "Ask for whatever you want me to give you."* [1 Chronicles 1:7]

## Devotion allows us to discover God's heart.

David's advice to Solomon was true. "If you seek Him, He will be found by you." With wholehearted devotion Solomon had sought for and found God. As a result, God offered Solomon anything he wanted.

Solomon's response revealed motives that were honorable in God's sight. His mind was set on God. In reply to God's offer, Solomon met the expectations outlined by his father David. Solomon's answer clearly shows a heart devoted to God.

*Solomon answered God, "You have shown great kindness to David my father and have made me king in his place. Now, LORD God, let your promise to my father David be confirmed, for you have made me king over a people who are as numerous as the dust of the earth. Give me wisdom and knowledge, that I may lead this people, for who is able to govern this great people of yours?"* [2 Chronicles 1:7-10]

Because of Solomon's devotion to God, he had a correct understanding of himself. Without God, he was nothing. Only out of God's kindness was he king over this great nation. He knew he needed what only God could give him if he would one day successfully complete the task of building God's temple and leading God's people to worship. Solomon needed God's wisdom and knowledge. Isn't it amazing? Solomon's devotion had taken him straight to the place he needed to be. Devotion had led Solomon to God's heart.

*God said to Solomon, "Since this is your heart's desire and you have not asked for wealth, riches, or honor, nor for the death of your enemies, and since you have not asked for a long life but for wisdom and knowledge to govern my people over whom I have made you king, therefore wisdom and knowledge will be given you. And I will also give you wealth, riches and honor, such as no king who was before you ever had and none after you will have."* [2 Chronicles 1:11-12]

> Devotion to God allows Him to accomplish His purpose in our lives.

What a response from God! Have you ever heard the saying, "You can't out give God"? This must be the best example of that truth. Solomon offered to God the only thing he had - a heart completely devoted to God's purposes. God responded in magnificence.

With God's blessing of wisdom and knowledge and material wealth never known before or since, Solomon led his people to build the temple. Using the blueprints given him by his father, Solomon personally supervised construction of the magnificent building that would be the abiding place of God's Spirit. With elegant gold and silver inlay, polished cedar panels, pine flooring, and incredible masses of stone, God's house was constructed. Only the best materials were used. No detail was overlooked. Solomon's wholehearted devotion was transformed into the place that Jehovah God would inhabit. Solomon's heart became God's abiding place.

As with Solomon, God has an expectation of devotion from each of us. With the ultimate position of authority our devotion will offer Him, God intends to accomplish His purpose in our lives just as He did with Solomon. Jesus explained God's expectation of devotion best.

*But seek first his kingdom and his righteousness, and all these things will be given to you as well.* [Matthew 6:33]

Solomon lived this truth hundreds of years before Jesus spoke the words. Today, centuries later, these words are still true.

By choosing devotion to God, Solomon gave God the appropriate place of authority in his heart. Consequently, God's presence allowed Solomon to recognize his own limitations. Then God led him to ask for what he needed most - wisdom and knowledge from Him. With a desire for God's leadership in his life, Solomon was poised for God's promise of abundance to be fulfilled.

God wants an intimate, personal relationship with each of us. For that to happen, we must desire Him. Above all else, in spite of all else, and in lieu of all else, God wants us to seek Him out, to know him. Ask God to instill in your heart a burning desire for Him. Then let God translate that desire into devotion.

> Devotion to God leads us toward allowing Him supremacy in our lives.

As we offer our lives in true devotion to God, we too will give God priority. With God in his rightful position, like Solomon, we will begin to see ourselves as we really are. Self examination in God's presence will reveal our shortcomings. Immediately, our list of needs will begin to change. As we continue to seek God, God's wisdom and knowledge will become the desire of our hearts. Then we, too, will be in line for God's abundance to be fulfilled in our lives.

A product of our devotion will be the desire to build a special dwelling place for God. Our temple will not be constructed with wood and stone, however. Our house will be built with love, obedience, confidence, devotion, patience, purity, submission, and commitment. You see, the place God desires to dwell is in our hearts. Through Jesus, God has made the provision for each of us to be His temple. Paul explained it in his letter to the Corinthians.

*Do you not know that your body is a temple of the Holy Spirit, who is in you, whom you have received from God? You are not your own; you were bought at a price. Therefore honor God with your body.* [1 Corinthians 6:19]

Like David, you have been given the responsibility of offering an example for your child to follow. Take a moment to examine your life. Are you seeking God with wholehearted devotion? Where is God on your list of priorities? Are you making your choices based on God's desires or do your choices reflect your own set of priorities? As you examine your heart, decide now to agree with God and accept his desires for you and your family. Give God the position of authority He deserves. Allow God to change your heart and change your mind so your desires will give way to God's purposes. This is the legacy your child deserves.

**From Parent to Teenager**: I want you to know of my absolute exuberant devotion to God. I want you to hear His praise coming from my lips. I want you to see my love for Him in my facial expressions. I want you to observe my devoted service to Him in the way I use my talents, read my Bible, and pray. I want you to experience my devotion to Him in the way I treat you and others. From me, my child, I want you to learn that devotion to God means giving Him first place.

## Rules to follow:
**Surrender you will to God's will.**
**Allow God to have supremacy in your life.**
**Discover God's heart through devotion to Him.**
**Find favor with God through devotion to Him.**


Father,
    Help me to learn to give you first place in my life. More than anything, Father, I want to seek you with wholehearted devotion. I want to know you, Lord. As I seek you first, change my heart and my mind about my sin. Help me to turn away from my sin and turn toward You. May your desires become my desire. May your purposes become my life. Grant me wisdom and understanding to do the job you have chosen for me to do. And Father, as I learn, help me teach my child to seek You with his whole heart. May my child see in me a heart completely devoted to You.

# Chapter Seven

## God Expects Submission
### Mary

*I am the Lord's servant, Mary answered. May it be to me as you have said.* [Luke 1:38]

There are many words whose earliest meanings have become adulterated over years of use. Many of these ideas have made complete circles through time to return, in some cases, to the original definition. Some changes have occurred over hundreds of years, progressing to a point and then stopping, resisting further change. Other words have slowly continued the path of change to a place so dramatic, the original intent cannot even be implied.

One word fitting this last characterization is *attitude*. The original intent of the word attitude was to offer a vehicle for the description of a person's perspective on an issue. The term was not associated with any pattern of good or evil. Nor was there an expectation of right or wrong. Attitude was simply used to relation position. To speak of a person's attitude was to describe his stance on a given issue. The suitability of the response added no value.

Through time, however, the term became allied with positive feedback. I am sure this association occurred as the powers that be, mothers and school teachers in particular, began to set the limits on what could be classified as an appropriate response to a given situation. As the concept of correct attitude evolved, so, too, evolved the connection between attitude and "good" behavior. This evolution can be seen as self perpetuating when one understands that no self respecting teacher or mother would freely tolerate any attitude other than a good one.

Then came the sixties. Overnight the word attitude became associated with defiance. For a person to have an attitude meant that person had been deemed a revolutionist. Attitude became the description of a person's negative feelings on the social disposition of our country. Having an attitude meant wanting society to change to one's own idea of conformity.

Through the seventies and eighties the negative connotation continued and expanded. Attitude became synonymous with any behavior of revolt. It seemed that children were being enlisted at birth to become members of a society perpetuating the idea that "good" and "attitude" were opposing thoughts. Parenting and teaching became sidelines while adjustments were made to accommodate the behavioral revolution that began to sweep our nation.

It was during this revolution that parents were duped into believing that the child was the most important part of the family. They were persuaded by a lot of psycho-babble to believe that children were just little adults whose thoughts and desires should be placed on equal footing with those of the adults in the family. These misinformed parents began to allow the well being of the family to revolve around the needs and wants of the child.

Soon, the child was elevated to "most favored being" status in the home. With this elevation in status, children began to expect "most favored being" treatment from their parents and from other adults. These ideas eventually led to a generation of petty, selfish little brats who constantly expected something for nothing and who believed with every fiber of their being that they should sit back and wait for what the world "owed" them. This behavioral revolution reached the bottom of the pit in 1989 and found our youngest child, Luke, waiting patiently in the muck.

Having barely escaped with his life his first year in school, Luke began the second grade with what seemed to be a determination to succeed. Our prayers had been answered when he was assigned to Mrs. Gillis' class. Not only is Myra an excellent teacher, she is also a pastor's wife. Tommy and I were pleased that Luke would be taught by someone sharing our values and beliefs. We were looking forward to a year free of conflict and disruption. Luke's approach to second grade was exemplary and lasted all of two days. In a matter of a few hours his attitude went from outstanding to revolting. For reasons which still escape me, Luke became convinced that his level of importance had taken an unexpected jump, placing him in a position of authority higher than his teacher. It seemed the conflict arose over Mrs. Gillis' requirements to complete daily class assignments on time. The need for cooperation from all her students was evident to everyone except our son.

Being the astute educator that she is, Mrs. Gills knew Luke's behavior had a root cause so she set out to identify the problem. First, she tried moving Luke to the front of the classroom. She was under the misconception that Luke was being distracted from his work and consequently was unable to complete all assignments in a timely fashion. Being fair, I would have to say that two days had not been enough time for Mrs. Gillis to evaluate Luke's attitude. By moving him, she was giving him the benefit of the doubt. Had she known at that time what she would soon learn about Luke, I am sure this trial would have been avoided. After two days, it became apparent his global positioning had no bearing on Luke's ability or desire to complete his work.

Next, Mrs. Gillis tried helping him with his skills of organization. She employed a kitchen timer to remind him of the deadline requirement. When each class assignment was made, Mrs. Gillis would set the clock for the allotted time and then remind Luke she was expecting completion of the task at hand before the time bell sounded. As a die-hard subversive, he routinely ignored Mrs. Gillis' warnings and continued to work at his own pace, often times never finishing anything.

After these and several other methods proved unsuccessful, Mrs. Gillis resorted to threatening Luke with a parent-teacher conference. Apparently, in his own feeble little mind, his elevation in status surpassed even his parent's authority since he was not at all concerned about the possibility that Mrs. Gillis would relate the details of his behavior to his father and me. When even this tactic failed to gain his cooperation, Mrs. Gillis was left with no alternative but to follow through with her threat.

Looking back on the situation, I now understand the problem was much broader than Luke's refusal to follow instructions and complete his assignments. The problem was also larger than his attitude. The real problem was that Luke had developed a pattern of behavior which excluded submission as a viable alternative. At the base of his refusal to cooperate was his belief that submission to a higher authority was not a necessity. Like many of us, Luke had never gained a correct understanding of submission. He did not realize that submission was the key to his personal well-being.

Luke is not alone in his error. Many people are confused

about the true meaning of submission. Some are under the misguided impression that submission means giving up. These people tend to see the act of submission as the final stage of failure, the place where no other alternative exists. Having tried for and failed to attain success through their own means, they are faced with only one choice - quitting. They stop trying as submission leaves them poised to accept their own inevitable failure.

Others view the act of submission as giving in. These are the people who believe submission requires an admission of wrongdoing. They believe to submit means that some other person or entity is more correct than they about a given situation. They view submission as a degradation of their self esteem. For these people, submission implies inferiority and inadequacy and a life of subservience.

But submission is not about giving up or giving in. Rather, true submission is simply acceptance and agreement. To submit means to accept the authority of a higher power and agree with the expectations that higher power has for you. To be submissive, the only thing we need to give up is our attitude; and complete freedom is all we must give in to. Because true submission ultimately leads us to God, it is always for our benefit. Submission becomes a way of life when we accept God's authority and agree with His expectations for our lives.

Like many of us, Luke, had not yet learned the value of true submission. Myra telephoned and explained the situation that had developed with our son. After listening intently to her predicament, I gave her the tool she needed to convince Luke it would be in his best interest to submit to her requests. You see, Luke had incorrectly judged his position and authority. He needed to be convinced that not only was there an authority higher than his, that authority had control over something he valued. Luke required the right incentive to develop an attitude of submission.

The next day when the class assignments were made,

Mrs. Gillis did not need to threaten Luke to gain his cooperation. Neither did she set the timer or move him to a new position in the classroom. What she did was offer Luke a valid reason to submit to her request. The conversation probably went something like this.

"Luke, I have explained to you the importance of completing your assignments on time. I have also tried several ways to help you reach this goal, but nothing has seemed to work. Because finishing your lessons on time is so important, from now on, you will not be allowed to go to lunch until all your assignments are completed. Do you understand?"

Are you curious about Luke's response? Let me assure you that he answered in the affirmative. As a matter of fact, I believe his exact words were, 'Yes, ma'am!"

Mrs. Gillis never had any trouble getting Luke to complete his work after that. You see, by illustrating her control over something Luke held near and dear to his heart - his food - Mrs. Gillis gave Luke a clear understanding of the personal benefit that comes from submission. Once Luke gained a clear understanding of true submission, he readily agreed to Mrs. Gillis's expectations for him.

> To what human authorities are you expected to submit? What happens when you refuse to be compliant? What are some things that submission is *not*? How is submission a good thing? Why are we afraid to be submissive to human authority? Why are we afraid to be submissive to God?

## Mary Submitted to God's Will

Mary was ecstatic. She and Joseph were officially engaged to be married. As was the custom, they would wait the requisite year to finalize their marriage, but that was just a formality. Their betrothal was set. Under Jewish law she was Joseph's wife and only divorce could separate the couple now.

Like every other teenager, Mary often let her thoughts wander freely. Many times while she was praying, she had thought about Isaiah's promise of a coming Messiah.

*Therefore the Lord himself will give you a sign: The virgin will be with child and will give birth to a son, and will call him Immanuel.* [Isaiah 7:14]

Just as every Jewish girl had done since the time of the prophets, Mary must have wondered who the mother of the Messiah would be. She knew in her heart that she qualified for the position, but probably dismissed the possibility since God would surely want someone from a more prominent family to be the mother of the King.

Who would be the mother of the Messiah? Would He be born during her lifetime? Would she get to see him? Would His mother be someone she knew? Only God could answer those questions. For the moment Mary was content to be engaged to Joseph and daydream about the life she would have with him.

Her heart soared when she thought about the way God had worked out the details of her life. For months she had prayed God would send her the perfect mate. She knew true happiness would come only with God's choice. Secretly, she had hoped for a kind, gentle man who would love her and the children she would bare. With Joseph, Mary knew God had intervened on her behalf and answered her prayers.

Mary was convinced her engagement to Joseph had not been the first time God had taken an active role in her family's life. The most recent intervention was with some of her family who lived in the hill country of Judea. Only a few months prior to the announcement of their engagement, Mary's mother had received word that one of Mary's relatives was pregnant.

Elizabeth and Zechariah had wanted children for many years, and now Elizabeth was expecting.

As Mary's family discussed the news over the evening meal, part of the details took on an unexplained significance for Mary. Both Elizabeth and Zechariah were well along in years, but that was not the astonishing part of this news. Neither was the fact that Elizabeth had been barren her entire life. What intrigued Mary was the account of Zechariah's service at the temple.

Something bizarre had occurred while Zechariah was offering incense. Mary wasn't sure exactly what had taken place, but when Zechariah had come out of the temple, he could not speak. It was only a short while later that Elizabeth discovered she was pregnant and went into seclusion. Even though she did not know the particulars, Mary knew that Zechariah's experience at the temple was connected with his wife's condition. She also knew that God had answered Elizabeth's prayer. What Mary did not know was that the angel Gabriel had appeared to Zechariah in the temple.

When Zechariah saw the angel, he was overcome with fear. Gabriel told him not to be afraid. He had come to bring good news. Zechariah's prayers for a child had been answered. Elizabeth would bear a son and Zechariah was to name him John.

The question must have shown in Zechariah's eyes. He and Elizabeth were too old to have children. Therefore, how could God accomplish what the angel had so boldly proclaimed when both he and his wife were unable to do their part?

When Zechariah voiced his question, it was apparent that his disbelief had covered his heart and blocked his view of God's sovereignty. How could he believe the angel's declaration when the physical evidence was stacked so overwhelmingly against the possibility?

Gabriel was offended. How dare this human question the authority of the Lord God Almighty in whose presence

Gabriel had stood. Because of his unbelief, God caused Zechariah to lose his ability to speak.

When Zechariah finally came out of the temple, everyone could see from his expression that something strange had taken place. Like one who had lost control of his sense, Zechariah's eyes were wide and his breathing labored. In one frantic motion, he clutched his throat, then turned to look back at the temple. His lips began to move but no sound was heard. The crowd hushed at the agonizing silence. Still the old priest struggled to speak.

Realizing he was mute but not paralyzed, Zechariah began to make signs with his hands. He waved his arms and pointed frantically at the temple, hoping to share his experience with the gathering throng. But his hands were not sufficient. He was mute and no feeble attempt at signing could relate the magnificence of his encounter with Gabriel. Finally, he gave up. It would not be until John's birth that Zechariah would regain his voice and be able to speak of his encounter with God's messenger.

Mary had thought about Elizabeth and Zechariah often since that evening at supper. Somehow she knew the day would come when she would understand the mystery behind Elizabeth's pregnancy. But for now, she contented herself with planning her marriage to Joseph. She could not remember ever feeling more blessed.

> God chooses the person He desires to receive His favor.

Mary had only just begun to think about the details of her marriage that day when she sensed a presence in her room. Turning quickly, she saw what appeared to be a man standing there. Before she could call out, the man spoke to her.

*"Greetings, favored one! The Lord is with you."* [Luke

1:28b]

What a strange thing for a strange man to say. And how did he sneak up on her? She had not heard one sound. While she was trying to get her thoughts together and decide whether to run, scream, or both, the stranger spoke again. Mary thought his voice sounded as calm as a summer breeze.

*"Do not be afraid, Mary, for you have found favor with God."* [Luke 1:30]

> God is able to answer our questions and calm our fears.

His soothing tone and his calm demeanor made Mary forget her fear.

How did this strange man know her innermost thoughts? He spoke of the very thing she had been contemplating since her betrothal to Joseph. She *had* found favor with God. That fact was evident in God's provision of Joseph to be her husband. Joseph was everything she had ever prayed for and more. Did this intruder think she needed to be reminded how blessed she was?

Just as that last thought passed through her brain, the stranger continued with the news that would rock Mary's world. As Gabriel spoke, Mary realized this messenger and this message were straight from God.

*And now, you will conceive in your womb and bear a son, and you will name him Jesus. He will be great, and will be called the son of the Most High, and the Lord God will give to him the throne of his ancestor David. He will reign over the house of Jacob forever, and of his kingdom there will be no end."* [Luke 1:31-33 NRSV]

While the angel was speaking, Mary's mind became a whirlwind of activity as she began contemplating the implications of his announcement. Even though she and Joseph were officially engaged, she was still a virgin and had planned to remain a virgin until her wedding night. Yet standing before her was an angel of God describing her role as the mother of the Messiah. Her child would be the Son of the Most High.

*Mary said to the angel, "How can this be, since I am a virgin?"* [Luke 1:34 NRSV]

> God gives assurance to the submissive heart.

Unlike Zechariah, Mary was not questioning the validity of the information Gabriel was imparting. Rather, she wanted insight. Mary knew her status. She had never been intimate with any man. She wanted to understand how God would accomplish His Word through her.

Because her heart was pure and her motives honorable, Gabriel explained to Mary how she would become pregnant and yet remain a virgin.

*The angel answered, "The Holy Spirit will come upon you, and the power of the Most High will overshadow you. So the holy one to be born will be called the Son of God. Even Elizabeth your relative is going to have a child in her old age, and she who was said to be barren is in her sixth month. For nothing is impossible with God."* [Luke 1:35-37]

Mary would be required to offer her heart, her mind, her entire being in submission to the will of God. So there would be no doubt in Mary's heart about God's intervention, Gabriel pointed out what she had already concluded. God's hand was on her life and the life of her family. Elizabeth was pregnant because God had willed it. This was the confirmation Mary needed.

Though Mary did not question God's control in these matters, Gabriel gave her the assurance that God would achieve this thing that seemed outside the realm of reality. With absolute certainty Gabriel stated, "Nothing is impossible with God." His final comment was more than just a declaration of God's ability. Mary needed to be comforted. Soon her mind would turn to the practical implications of his news. Gabriel knew she would need to find solace in God's control over her life.

Mary's mind reeled with excitement! She was to become pregnant by the Holy Spirit. So that was how a virgin would conceive and bare a son! She was going to be the mother of the Messiah. This was almost too much to believe. As she contemplated the news Gabriel had offered, her thoughts quickly turned to her betrothed. What would Joseph think? How would she ever explain to him that she had not been unfaithful? What would his parents say? What would her parents say? How would the neighbors react?

> Have your ever been faced with a situation in which submission to God went against public opinion? Has He asked something of you which meant that if you submitted to His will, you would find yourself at odds with those around you?

Suddenly, Mary realized the problem was larger than just what someone else might think. She could be facing legal consequences. Was her situation addressed in the Book of the Law? As she responded to her own silent question, she realized the truth. The law was clear. Pregnancy without the benefit of marriage was addressed in the Book of the Law and as Mary considered what the law had to say, her breath must have caught in her throat.

*If there is a young woman, a virgin already engaged to be married, and a man meets her in the town and lies with her, you shall bring both of them to the gate of that town and stone them to death, the young woman because she did not cry for help in the town and the man because he violated his neighbor's wife. So you shall purge the evil from your midst.* [Deuteronomy 22:23-24 NRSV]

The law left no alternative. Mary, the teenager this angel had just declared *favored of God,* was facing certain death. How could her life have changed so quickly? One moment she had been anticipating her future with Joseph and the next, she was absorbing the news that she was chosen by God to be the mother of the Messiah. In an instant Mary had gone from planning her wedding to contemplating her death. Gabriel waited patiently for Mary's response.

As the haze cleared and Mary began to think with her heart, she was calmed by a peace only God can give. She raised her head to look at Gabriel. Her expression conveyed what she believed. Gabriel could see that Mary knew what she needed to do. He was pleased that Mary understood the importance of submission. Even though saying "yes" to God could lead to her death, Mary could not say "no".

| God gives freedom to the submissive heart. |

When she spoke, Mary demonstrated the correct attitude one should have toward God. First, she willingly accepted God's authority over her life. Without reservations she acknowledged that God was in control. Even though Gabriel's announcement detailed a turn of events this teenager had never anticipated, she was prepared to give herself in service to the Lord.

Second, Mary readily agreed with God's

expectations for her life. God's plan was not even remotely similar to the one formulated by Mary and Joseph. Yet, Mary quickly realized that without God their plans were meaningless anyway. Even though what God desired was completely impossible from her perspective, Mary was confident that God would accomplish what He had said.

With her response, Mary let us view a heart filled with freedom that comes with true submission.

*Then Mary said, "Here am I, the servant of the Lord; let it be with me according to your word." Then the angel departed from her.* [Luke 1:38 NRSV]

Mary submitted to God's authority and agreed to His expectations, but she still faced many trials before God's plan could be accomplished. How would she explain to Joseph? Was their love strong enough to withstand the questions he would have? Would her betrothed believe that an angel had visited her and would he still want her? As she wondered about these questions, Mary may have taken solace in the truth that eludes many of us a lifetime - God never leaves anything to chance.

> God is in control of every situation.

When Joseph learned of Mary's condition he was crushed. How could she expect him to believe the story about an angel? He loved her, but he could not accept an unfaithful wife. As she cried and pleaded with him, Joseph knew she had begun to believe her own story. He could see in her eyes that she was convinced she carried the Messiah in her womb. Poor Mary. Poor Joseph. Joseph's love for her was not enough to overcome his hurt.

The pain he felt seemed to crush the life from his heart. Still, he did not want Mary to suffer. He refused to have her judged publicly. Joseph knew he could easily arrange for their divorce by quietly signing the necessary legal papers. Mary would never need to face public scrutiny. He would see to that.

Her heart ached with her love for Joseph. She knew his kindness would prevent her death, but she wanted more. Mary wanted Joseph to believe her. She wanted him to understand that God had to be first in her life. She wanted Joseph to know that submission was the only choice her heart could make.

Having taken the time to think through the entire matter, Joseph was convinced that he understood the problem. He believed the problem was protecting Mary from the shame of public disgrace. He was wrong. No matter how much Joseph analyzed the circumstances, he could not comprehend the true dilemma.

As Joseph was considering the best way to accomplish the divorce, once again God intervened.

*But after he had considered this, an angel of the Lord appeared to him in a dream and said, "Joseph, son of David, do not be afraid to take Mary home as your wife, because what is conceived in her is from the Holy Spirit."* [Matthew 1:20]

The real problem was not Mary or her pregnancy, but rather Joseph's fear. Like us, Joseph was afraid to believe God even when believing was the easiest thing to do. Why was Joseph afraid to believe God? Was it because he could not accept that God wanted to include him in a miracle?

How many times have we questioned God because what He seemed to want from us skirted on the edge of the impossible? Are we like Joseph? Are we comfortable believing God only for the common things? When an impossible task confronts us, do we forget or ignore God's sovereignty? We readily accept those things from God which are possible from our perspective, but we balk when God wants to do an impossible work in us. When will we understand that God operates from a perspective different than our own? When our efforts are doomed to certain failure, God can succeed without effort.

*She will give birth to a son, and you are to give him the name Jesus, because he will save his people from their sins."* [Matthew 1:21]

The angel did more for Joseph than confirm Mary's story. The angel also gave Joseph additional information which bound his heart to Mary's unborn son. The name Joseph was to give God's son had a special meaning. The child would be called Jesus because he would be the Savior -- Mary's Savior, Joseph's Savior. This baby would be the salvation for their people.

The angel continued by explaining to Joseph why his quiet, simple life had taken this unexpected turn.

*All this took place to fulfill what the Lord had said through the prophet: "The virgin will be with child and will give birth to a son, and they will call him Immanuel" --which means, "God with us."* [Matthew 1:22-23]

The child carried by Mary would be God in the flesh. Suddenly everything fell into place. Joseph would rear the Son of God. He, Joseph, a simple carpenter from Nazareth, would be used of God for the fulfillment of prophecy. God's Word was true. A virgin *had* conceived and *would* bear a son! It was a miracle and Joseph was a part of the miracle! If Joseph could count on nothing else, from that moment forward he knew he could depend on the Word of the LORD.

---
Submission to the LORD means following Him all the way.
---

*When Joseph woke up, he did what the angel of the LORD had commanded him and took Mary home as his wife. But he had no union with her until she gave birth to a son. And he gave him the name Jesus.* [Matthew 1:24-25]

Isn't it amazing how our outlook can change after God pays us a visit? Our judgment can be so clouded that we are unable to see the truth when it is right before our eyes. Then God intervenes and we gain clarity of vision. With God's help any of us can renew our perspective. Is it not worth the time to listen to God's point of view since all things are possible with God?

God not only gives sight, he also gives insight. Through His instruction we are able to discover the real problems that face us. In doing so, He helps us identify the changes our hearts must undergo so that His plans can be accomplished. As we get a glimpse of our own hearts, submission becomes our only alternative. God's goals then become our goals. God's heart then becomes our heart.

The young couple waited anxiously as the time of Mary's delivery drew near. For months they had thought about all of the things Gabriel had told them. Neither Mary nor Joseph had spoken of the visitation by the angel to anyone else. They both knew, without speaking it, this was one birth announcement God would see to personally.

Just when things seemed to be settling down, the Roman Emperor sent out an edict that would change everything for the young couple.

*In those days a decree went out from Emperor Augustus that all the world should be registered. This was the first registration and was taken while Quirinius was governor of Syria. All went to their own towns to be registered. Joseph also went from the town of Nazareth in Galilee to Judea, to the city of David called Bethlehem, because he was descended from the house and family of David. He went to be registered with Mary, to whom he was engaged and who was expecting a child. [Luke 2:1-5 NRSV]*

Leave it to the government to throw a wrench in the works. Mary was very close to delivering and, like any young husband, Joseph was frantic with worry. Having a baby is difficult enough, but now, due to the Emperor's edict, the young couple would need to travel to Bethlehem before the baby was born. How much more could Mary stand? With his confidence in the One who controlled their destiny, Joseph had no alternative but to put Mary on the back of a burro and head down to Bethlehem for the registration.

Bethlehem was in complete confusion. Never before had the little town seen so much activity and so many visitors. Even when David was alive, Bethlehem had never been this crowded. People and animals were everywhere. Everyone was related to everyone else since they were all descendants of King David. As such, they had come to put their names on the Roman government's tax roles. Some had traveled further than Joseph and Mary, but none were as tired. All Joseph wanted was to find a place for Mary to be comfortable for the night.

Earlier in the day Mary had felt the first twinges of labor. She had remained silent. The last thing Joseph needed was another problem. She knew he was already under tremendous pressure to get her to Bethlehem before nightfall and she did not want to add to his worry. Mary was certain her husband would not have continued their journey to Bethlehem had he realized her labor had begun.

Mary had learned much about Joseph in the last few months. After the angel had spoken to him in a dream, he had come to her and apologized for mistrusting her. She knew how difficult this must have been for him. Her heart sang with joy as she watched him overcome his doubts.

Now as they were approaching Bethlehem, Mary found

strength in knowing that Joseph had learned to trust the LORD completely. He was once again the kind, gentle man she had first met. He would be the best human father her son could have.

By the time they arrived in Bethlehem, Mary's labor had progressed to the last stages. Stopping at the first inn inside the city gates, Joseph was devastated to learn there were no rooms available anywhere in the city. Wishing he did not have to disappoint Mary with more bad news, he stepped outside. Before he could speak, he saw in her eyes that her time had come. How could he tell her there were no rooms available?

Looking back at the innkeeper, he silently pleaded for help. The innkeeper saw Mary's distress and directed the young couple to a cave behind his small inn. Sleeping with the animals was better than staying out in the night.

Even though the accommodations were much less than Joseph had wanted, Mary was glad to have a place to lie down. By carefully spreading woven blankets atop some fresh hay, Joseph arranged a makeshift bed for his wife. He then helped Mary from the back of the donkey. As she rested on the straw, Mary was once again comforted by Gabriel's words: "For nothing is impossible with God."

> Submission does not guarantee an easy path - but it does guarantee the presence of God.

Looking back, Mary could see the intricate detail of God's hand on her life. Submission had not been the easiest route, but Mary knew God had been in constant attendance. Now as she awaited the birth of the Christ child, she felt God's presence even more. Mary gained comfort in thinking of the miraculous way God had taken her meager offering of submission and formulated a magnificent plan for man's redemption. Her baby would be more than another king. He would be the King of Kings. Her child was God's son and he would save the people from their sins.

*While they were there, the time came for her to deliver her child. And she gave birth to her firstborn son and wrapped him in bands of cloth, and laid him in a manger, because there was no place for them in the inn.* [Luke 2:6-7 NRSV]

That night, in a stable surrounded by livestock, Mary's submission culminated in the birth of God's perfect love. Because Mary understood God's authority over her life and accepted God's expectations, she became the bearer of God's love to the world. By making the choice to be submissive, Mary positioned herself to achieve God's best. Mary understood submission and became a perfect example for each of us.

As Mary wrapped her baby and leaned back against the fresh hay, God prepared to announce the Savior's birth. I can only imagine the excitement that flowed from wingtip to wingtip as the angles lined up to herald the birth. What a press release this was going to be! Nothing known to man can even imitate the power under control that evening. Like a volcano ready to blow, the anticipation mounted to the point of explosion. Then God sent out his first evangelist.

In fields very near the stable were shepherds tending their flocks. Suddenly, out of nowhere, a light burst forth from the heavens. This was not an ordinary white light, but a light alive with the splendor of a spectrum of color. Pulsating with an energy never witnessed by man, the light exploded with joy, then swirled to regain composure. With unimaginable speed, the pinpoint of light ricocheted across the sky, bouncing from star to star. Powered by uncontrolled jubilation, the brilliance gained force as it bounded haphazardly from one point in the universe to the next.

---
Submission to the instructions of the LORD insures great blessings.
---

One of the shepherds had barely opened his mouth to call out to the others when he looked up and saw the light coming straight toward him. The sound lodged in his throat. Able only to point, the shepherd watched as the point of brilliance advanced at full speed. With coordinates locked in on a predetermined course, the light sped toward the shepherds and then abruptly stopped, lingering in the sky above them.

Thinking a collision was imminent, the shepherds fell to the ground. The instinct of survival made them cover their heads with their hands as though that would offer some protection. Moments passed before the shepherds realized the light had screeched to a halt directly above them.

Looking up, the group saw a massive being standing in the center of the light. Suspended in mid-air, the creature hovered above the shepherds. No part of him touched the ground and yet he did not waver with effort. Afraid of any being that could accomplish a feat like they had all witnessed, the shepherds remained on the ground, terrified of what might happen next.

It must have been Gabriel. Surely God would have allowed him to complete this mission that had begun with his visit to Zechariah. As an angel who spent time in the presence of God, Gabriel would have had a supply of God's glory sufficient to offer the display the shepherds had witnessed that evening. And with the memory of Mary's submission fresh in his thoughts, Gabriel's joy would have been a natural overflow of praise to the Lord.

As the shepherds waited, fearing what would happen next, the angel spoke.

*But the angel said to them, "Do not be afraid; for see--I am bringing you good news of great joy for all the people: to you is born this day in the city of David a Savior, who is the Messiah, the Lord. This will be a sign for you: you will find a child wrapped in bands of cloth and lying in a manger."* [Luke

2:10-12 NRSV]

For the shepherds, it was more than good news. It was great news! You see, the shepherds knew their place in society. They were at the bottom. Because their jobs demanded their constant presence with the animals, they were never considered clean. They were not allowed to participate in the religious ceremonies. The shepherds tended the animals that would be sacrificed, but that was where their involvement ended.

But now things had changed. Not only would they survive this scare, the shepherds were a part of this group for whom the Messiah had come! **All** people. The angel had said **ALL**. This would be one time when the shepherds would not be excluded. No one was excluded! Even the lowliest of the low would be able to partake in this blessing from God.

*And suddenly there was with the angel a multitude of the heavenly host, praising God and saying, "Glory to God in the highest heaven, and on earth peace among those whom he favors!"* [Luke 2:10-12 NRSV]

They appeared out of nowhere. Without warning the shepherds were surrounded by thousands of angelic beings all intent on the same purpose - paying tribute to the LORD God Most High. The sound was tremendous. No acoustical adjustments were necessary for this concert. With their voices joined in unison of praise, the angels gave the shepherds their first glimpse of heaven.

Fear can find no place in the company of heaven's hosts. The shepherds stood with confidence. No longer were they afraid. They were included! It was their peace with God about which the angels spoke. They were now favored of God. As they watched, the angels continued to lift their voices in a litany of praise unequaled in time. Jesus was born! The Savior had come! Hallelujah! Hallelujah! Hallelujah!

*When the angels had left them and gone into heaven, the shepherds said to one another, "Let us go now to Bethlehem and see this thing that has taken place, which the Lord has made known to us." So they went with haste and found Mary and Joseph, and the child lying in the manger. When they saw this, they made known what had been told them about this child; and all who heard it were amazed at what the shepherds told them. But Mary treasured all these words and pondered them in her heart. The shepherds returned, glorifying and praising God for all they had heard and seen, as it had been told them.* [Luke 2:15-29 NRSV]

There are two things a shepherd never does. He never gets in a hurry and he never leaves his flock unattended. Sheep are jittery creatures and always react best to a calm spirit and slow, deliberate movement. A flurry of activity frightens the animals and causes them to scatter. Left unattended, they can be attacked by predators. The animals have no defense mechanism sufficient to protect themselves from a hungry attacker. For the sheep to remain safe, the shepherd must constantly stand guard. (Sounds a little like us, doesn't it?)

On the hills outside of Bethlehem that night, when God revealed His love to the shepherds, not only did they leave their sheep, they left in a hurry. The shepherds ran to meet Jesus! I never cease to be amazed at the impact God's revelation of love can have on a person. The shepherds immediately wanted to be a part of that love. They dropped everything to go and see their Savior face to face. Not only that, after they had seen the baby they immediately began to tell everyone they met. They were eager to share what they had discovered. Without regard for public opinion or personal goals, the shepherds made known what had been told them about the child. And guess what? People listened and were amazed at what the shepherds had to say.

**Parent to Teenager:** As a direct result of Mary's submission, God's love was revealed to man. It is through submission that you will become a vehicle for the revelation of God's love to others. God does expect submission. Submission to God is for your benefit.

## Rules to follow:

**Accept God's authority in your life because God wants what is best for you.**
**Learn to agree with God's expectations even when you do not fully understand God's plan.**
**Trust that God's love for you will be sufficient.**
**Know that God will always be with you.**

Father,
Help me to be submissive to You. As I learn, help me teach my child. Give me the peace to know that Your plan is the best plan for my life. Help me accept Your authority over me and find comfort in my position. As I accept Your authority, help me agree with your expectations for my life. More than anything, Father, I want to be a bearer of Your love to the world.

# Chapter Eight

## God Expects Commitment
### Jesus

*Didn't you know I had to be in my Father's house?*
[Luke 2:49b]


Only after the birth of our third child did I truly begin to appreciate the robin's view of child rearing.

It was the morning of the first Saturday of summer after Luke had finished second grade. I had just poured my second cup of coffee and retired to the back porch when I noticed a bird's nest where I least expected. Nestled securely between the leaves of the artificial plant in my white plastic planter was a tiny nest with three gaping mouths poised in expectation of their next meal.

As I sat on the steps, I watched the mother and father bird

swoop into place on the edge of the nest and gently drop tiny morsels of food into the waiting mouths. Trip after long trip, they worked diligently to find the food and then return it to their waiting chicks.

Over the next several weeks I continued to watch the pair raise their brood. As I observed their parenting skills, I realized the robins' actions were very much akin to the routine my husband and I had fallen into in caring for our children, with one major difference -- the robins never had to chase their chicks down in order to feed them! They had been smart enough to build an enclosure that kept the chicks bunched together until that fateful day when they would give them the boot!

The advantage of a restricted rearing area was almost lost on me until the day it took three magnets to hold all the summer league ball schedules on our refrigerator. The time for our discussion on being committed to the end of the season, no matter what the circumstances, had long since passed. All three children had accepted our challenge and were members of separate teams. As Tommy and I glanced over the three different schedules, we enjoyed a momentary embrace, and then waved good-bye for the summer.

Those of you with only one child will never be able to appreciate the logistics nightmare we faced that summer. Most of Dave's and Luke's games were at different fields. To make matters worse, K'Anna's games were usually at a third complex.

It was on one of those evenings when the boys' teams were scheduled to play at different times and at different fields that I first began to gain a clear understanding of the importance of commitment.

Dave's game was set for 6 p.m. in Florence. Luke had a 7 o'clock game in Richland, about five miles north. K'Anna's team had an open date. After careful planning we decided that I would accompany Dave to his game in Florence. Afterwards, the two of us would join the rest of the family at Luke's game.

Everything went according to plan, but Dave and I

arrived at Luke's game just a few minutes too late to see him play. Just as we were driving up, Luke's coach replaced him in the line-up.

Expecting to see my eight-year-old dejected because his playing time had been cut short, I was surprised when I stepped up to the back of the dug-out and saw him engaged in an animated conversation with a team mate.

"Hey, Mom," Luke said as he turned toward me, "You should have seen it! I was great!"

Knowing Luke's propensity for flamboyance should have kept me evenly keeled, but it did not. As I watched the glee on his small face, I knew I would respond so that he would feel free to share his latest adventure with me.

"Great!" I countered. "You were great! Tell me what I missed, Luke."

Needing no more encouragement, Luke stood, picked up his bat, and turned toward me as he exclaimed, "I almost hit a home run!"

"Really?" I was suddenly as animated as Luke. "You *really* almost hit a home-run?"

"Really and truly," he stated emphatically as he nodded with great exaggeration.

I couldn't believe my ears. Maybe our assumption that due to his size and build, Luke's sport would eventually be football had been a little premature. Maybe we were raising another "Babe"!

As I enjoyed Luke's excitement I noticed a look of surprise on his teammate's face. Then, without warning, the other boy jumped up and ran full force toward Luke, skidding to a stop just before reaching him. The boy gave Luke a quick elbow punch to the ribs as he shouted, "You didn't almost hit a home run, Luke!"

"I did too," was Luke's immediate retort.

"No you didn't, Luke. You struck out!"

As the truth of the matter slowly penetrated my reverie,

Luke's response became the basis for my understanding of true commitment.

Without a moment's hesitation, Luke explained. "Yep, I struck out. But if I had hit that ball, it would have gone over the fence!"

With just a few simple words from the heart of an eight-year-old, my thinking about commitment changed forever. From that moment on I knew that real commitment means staying true to your course and meeting every challenge while always expecting the best possible outcome.

> In a lifetime, a person makes many commitments. There are the commitments of engagement - such as, *I will be in a certain place at a certain time.* There are commitments of promise - as to a marriage or other important undertaking. There are commitments which involve a promise or a pledge. There are commitments to duties and to other people. And there is the commitment a person makes to God. Search your life and think about the commitment you have made to Him. Write that commitment on a card and place it in your Bible. Read it often.

## Jesus Lived a Life of Total Commitment

It is an awesome responsibility for me to presume to offer possible thought patterns for another mother, especially the mother of Jesus. However, I *am* a mother and I can identify with the perspective Mary might have had on the events in the life of her son. As a mother, I can make the case for the commitment of Jesus to God's plan as viewed and understood through Mary's eyes.

Apart from God the Father, only Mary had an insight into

the commitment of Jesus. Only Mary held in her heart the conversation with Gabriel about the child she would bear. Only Mary was present for His glorious birth and His bitter death. As they gathered around the cross, only Mary had recollection of Jesus as a twelve-year-old committed to the work of the Father.

Mary's own commitment to God's plan as she watched her Son live and die became the underlying superstructure that makes commitment an attainable goal for me - for all of us.

> **Our commitment to God should be evident to our children.**

From the moment of Gabriel's announcement, Mary became committed to allowing God's will to be worked in her life and in the life of her son.

When God told Joseph in a dream to take Mary and Jesus to Egypt in order to avoid Herod's death threat against him, she and Joseph obeyed without question. When it was safe to do so, the young couple went to Nazareth, Mary's hometown, again in obedience to God's direction. From these early experiences, Jesus was exposed to the dedication to God of the two who would rear him - Mary, the young virgin chosen by God to bring the Son of God into the world, and her husband, Joseph, the carpenter.

The Feast of Unleavened Bread was always a hectic time, and Mary knew the year Jesus was twelve years old would certainly be no different. Thousands of people began to converge on Jerusalem days before the week long celebration was scheduled to begin. Finding lodging was a nightmare if you had no relatives living inside the walls. Those visitors without a place to stay were left with no alternative but to camp in large groups on the hills surrounding the city.

Merchants from around the world gathered with their wares in open markets. Any item needed for the week long celebration of the Exodus could be found. From sacrificial animals to grains to beautifully dyed cloth -- Jerusalem had it all. The merchants always flocked to Jerusalem during the week of the Passover celebration because it was the most productive week of their year. Where else could a merchant find such a great concentration of people, all gathered for the same purpose?

For the devout Jew, the Feast was much more than a marketing opportunity. As one of the three yearly celebrations requiring attendance of all Jewish males, the Feast of Unleavened Bread was a special time of remembrance and thanksgiving. Since the days of their exodus from Egypt almost fifteen hundred years earlier, God's people had stopped each year to honor His deliverance of their firstborn from the angel of death. For the nation of Israel, this was a special week of sacrifice, worship, and reflection. More than any other, this was the one week each year when every Jewish family wanted to honor God by worshiping at the temple.

The Passover meal was the official start of the Feast of Unleavened bread. The celebration was a family affair. Typically the entire family would travel to Jerusalem, arriving several days before the fifteenth day of Nisan, the official beginning of the feast. Because the Jews marked time from sunset to sunset, the feast actually began at sunset on the fourteenth.

On the fourteenth day of the month, each family sacrificed a lamb as a part of their purification ceremony. Later that day the animal was roasted and preparations made for the evening meal. As the sun set on the fourteenth day of the month of Nisan, the family gathered to eat the Passover meal.

Before the meal began, the story of the Exodus was told as prescribed by Scripture.

*On that day tell your son, 'I do this because of what the LORD did for me when I came out of Egypt.'* [Exodus 13:8]

The head of the family then introduced the feast by

holding up a goblet of wine and reciting a praise to God for the deliverance of God's people out of bondage.

In addition to the roasted lamb, bitter herbs were eaten in memory of the ordeals suffered by the Jews in Egypt. Unleavened bread was also served to remind the people of the bread baked in haste before leaving Egypt. In total, the Passover was the beginning of a week long celebration of Jewish freedom.

> Our commitment to God requires obedience to His Word.

Although the trip from Nazareth to Jerusalem was a long journey, especially when traveling with young children, Jesus lived in a home that was committed to keeping the Law.

Although his mother, when she thought about that trek, might have cringed at the potential problems she and Joseph could face, they nevertheless made preparations for the trip to Jerusalem where they would worship at the temple.

For days in advance of their departure, Jesus probably watched as Mary gathered all the things her family would need for their trip, smiling as she busied herself with her work and thought about the journey she and Joseph had made just twelve years earlier.

After the angel had appeared to her with the wonderful news that she would give birth to the Messiah, their lives had quickly changed. Joseph, at first skeptical of Mary's story, had a change of heart after welcoming an angelic visitor into his dreams one night. Mary had quickly forgiven Joseph for mistrusting her. After all, her story was more than far fetched if the reality of divine intervention was not considered. When Joseph had shared his dream with her, Mary knew that somehow everything would be all right.

Jesus knew that Joseph's acceptance of God's plan became a point of security for Mary. And boy, were there moments during her pregnancy when Mary needed to feel secure.

Just the normal problems of pregnancy would have been enough. But added to that, Mary and Joseph had to deal with the reaction of the community.

Having lived in a small, tight-knit Jewish community her entire life, Mary's worst bouts of insecurity had come each time she was given a side long glance by one of her childhood friends. She had often shared her dreams for marriage and family with the other young girls in her group. Like them, she had protected the purity she would bring to her husband. She had looked forward to an engagement and then marriage to a good man of her family's choosing.

But after the angel's visit, Mary had become the object of scorn by her friends. To make matters worse, as much as Mary longed to share her good fortune with them, she knew they would never accept the reality of God's plan for her. Now, twelve years later, Mary smiled to herself as she realized how God's purpose had replaced the need for her neighbor's acceptance. Mary had contented herself knowing that through divine intervention God would see to it that His plan was fulfilled.

And things had turned out perfectly. Every time Mary took a moment to remember the events surrounding Jesus' birth at Bethlehem, she marveled at the way God had cared for her little family. Sometimes she would laugh out loud as she remembered the look on the faces of those shepherds. They didn't know whether to laugh or cry. Mary instinctively knew they must have seen Gabriel, but they were so busy talking to each other and telling Joseph about their encounter with the angel, she never had the chance to tell them that she too had met the huge creature.

Then, as they saw the child lying in the feed trough, they grew quiet and their faces reflected the wonder of God's presence. Their reaction to her baby had moved Mary to tears. As she and Joseph watched, each shepherd seemed compelled to touch the infant. Gently, the callused hands reached out to stroke the head of her new born. With each touch the men were changed.

Mary had often thought about the love she had seen in the

eyes of each shepherd. From the youngest to the oldest, they all seemed to know her baby. With a reverence and an awe she had never before witnessed, the shepherds had worshiped her son. As they left that night, Mary could hear their voices echoing across the night sky. "The Savior is born. We have seen him. The Messiah has come."

It had been months later that Joseph casually mentioned to Mary the appearance of a bright star on the horizon. Each evening the two had searched the skies for the star. With each passing night, the star had gained brilliance as it made its way toward them. Joseph and Mary watched together as the star continued to inch its way across the sky until finally, it found a permanent station above their home.

It was not until Mary looked out across the landscape a few days later that she began to comprehend the star's significance. There on the farthest hill, Mary saw what looked to be a caravan. As she squinted her eyes against the feigning light of dusk, she saw men of obvious wealth leading the entourage. Silhouetted against the evening sky, the group moved at a steady pace, looking toward the star that was now a constant fixture above her home.

Still unsure of their purpose, Mary caught a glimpse of the joy overflowing their hearts as they pointed toward the star that hovered above her. Suddenly Mary knew the purpose of their journey. These men were searching for her son.

As she stepped aside, one by one the men moved forward to bow before Jesus. What a memory! Her heart had soared as she realized God's plan of salvation would include even the Gentiles. What she witnessed as these men fell on their faces before her son was nothing short of miraculous. Never before or since had she seen anything to equal the majesty of that moment. As they bowed before her child, the men presented gifts to celebrate their joy over finding the Christ -- gold, frankincense, and myrrh. All gifts fit for a king.

After the men paid homage to the child, they spoke to

Mary of their journey. Mary had marveled at their faith in God's plan as she listened to their story. Though not of Jewish descent, they were all students of the Scripture and were familiar with the prophecies about the events surrounding the birth of the Messiah. When the star had risen in their sky, they had recognized its significance. Wanting desperately to see the Messiah, the men had set out on the journey that would cover thousands of miles before it ended.

For what must have been the hundredth time, Mary wondered if the foreigners ever learned of the massacre their visit to Herod had prompted. Upon their arrival in Israel, the foreigners had traveled first to Jerusalem. They had probably reasoned the capitol city of the Jewish nation was a good starting point in their quest to find the King of the Jews. Surely they could not have known that their query about the birth of a new king would eventually lead to the fulfillment of the prophecy of Jeremiah.

*This is what the LORD says: "A voice is heard in Ramah, mourning and great weeping, Rachel weeping for her children and refusing to be comforted, because her children are no more."* [Jeremiah 31:15]

Mary had cried when she heard the estimates. One would have been too many, but there had been between twenty and thirty-five babies killed. For Herod, only one mattered. Each child was less that two years of age since Herod wanted to destroy only those born since the appearance of the star. All were massacred as part of Herod's unsuccessful attempt to assassinate the new king.

Once again, God had protected Mary's family. Before Herod's plan could be accomplished, Joseph was warned by an angel to take Jesus and Mary and go to Egypt. Financially secure due to the gifts offered by the foreigners, Joseph, Mary, and Jesus were on their way to safety when the massacre took place.

After they had been in Egypt for a while, another of God's messengers appeared to Joseph in a dream. It was time to go home. Herod was dead and Jesus would be safe. Because the son of Herod the Great had taken over as the new Judean ruler, Joseph did not feel secure returning to the area around Bethlehem. So he led his family into the northern district of Galilee.

Now, more than ten years later, Mary and her family were in Nazareth where they had settled upon their return from Egypt. Like thousands of their countrymen, they were making preparations to travel to Jerusalem for the Passover. Mary could not have known the impact this trip would have on their lives as she watched her twelve-year-old help his father load the pack animals.

With several weeks' provisions, Joseph and his family headed toward the Holy City. Like every Passover trip in years past, the older children seemed to gather in groups along the great caravan of people making their way to the capitol city. At twelve, Jesus was now old enough to join his friends.

Each morning as Joseph watched his son leave their camp to join his friends, he would marvel at how much the boy had grown in the last few years. It seemed like only yesterday he had watched the young child as he bounded joyously around the shop where Joseph earned his living as a carpenter. Then later, as Jesus had begun his training in the Scriptures, Joseph had been amazed at the boy's understanding of the Law. Never before had Joseph seen a young mind so eager to know the things of God. Now, as Jesus approached his teenage years, Joseph could sense another change in the making.

Joseph had never misunderstood his role in Jesus' life. Not one time since the first visit from an angelic messenger had Joseph questioned God's purpose for him. Joseph knew his primary responsibility was to see to the well-being of the Messiah. He had been committed to that task, and, without pause, he had worked diligently to protect and to provide for God's Son.

Joseph loved Jesus as much as he loved the children who

had been born to him and Mary. As he watched him leave with his friends that day, tears of joy threatened to spill down Joseph's cheeks. Wiping his eyes, he looked up to the sky. In silence he offered a "thank you" for the opportunity to participate in the life of the Savior.

Jerusalem was chaotic, but Joseph and Mary were committed to battling the crowds to offer their sacrifice at the temple. After the purification ceremony, they prepared and enjoyed the Passover meal as prescribed in the Book of Law. Joseph led his family in thanksgiving as they remembered God's deliverance of their people from Egyptian bondage.

At twelve, Jesus was only one year away from taking his rightful place in the Jewish religious community. This year, like none before, Jesus had paid special attention to the ceremonies associated with the feast. More than that, however, he seemed enthralled with the teachers in the temple courts. For hours upon end he sat and listened as the rabbis read and explained the Scripture. Joseph and Mary had never seen anything like it.

As the week of celebration drew to an end, the throngs of people who had converged on Jerusalem slowly began to make their way back home. Joseph and Mary said goodbye to friends and family they would not see for another year. Jesus had left early that morning as they were loading the last of their belongings. Neither Joseph nor Mary was concerned about Jesus as they slowly began to make their way north out of the city. They were confident he would catch up with them by nightfall.

But dusk came and went and Jesus was nowhere to be found. After questioning the other families who had left Jerusalem that day, the couple knew Jesus had never left the city. With a night's rest, they turned around and headed back to Jerusalem in search of their son.

The journey back into the city was more difficult as they moved against the stream of people leaving after the Passover. Often times having to leave the road to make room for the oncoming traffic, Joseph and Mary continued at a slow but steady pace back toward the city. They questioned each new group they met and each gave them the same answer. No. No one had seen a twelve-year-old boy looking for his parents.

Though hindered by exhaustion, Joseph and Mary entered the city gates and continued the search for their son. Trying the homes of family first, then friends, they searched in vain until darkness overcame them. They were left with no other choice but to postpone their efforts until morning. With the first light of day, the two set out to scour the streets, looking for any clue of Jesus' whereabouts.

> Our commitment to God produces a desire to learn and to teach others.

Late that afternoon, they stumbled upon him. There, in the temple courts where he had been for three days, Mary and Joseph found their son. Sitting among the teachers, Jesus had spent the time listening, asking, and answering questions. His understanding of the Scriptures was astounding. Everyone who had heard Jesus was astonished that a twelve-year-old child could be so accomplished in the law.

Joseph and Mary were caught between a rock and a hard place. Both must have been proud of the way Jesus was handling himself with the teachers of the Law. Seeing him there must have been like watching your piano student sneak a practice session at Carnegie Hall. But his parents' pride in his advanced understanding of the Scripture did not change the fact that they had spent three days in anguish, searching everywhere for him.

Initially shocked by the scene they witnessed, Mary was the first to speak. Like any parent caught in a similar position, Mary set about to chastise Jesus. Careful not to draw attention away from the good Jesus was doing, she wanted him to understand the anxiety they had felt at his absence. Because the most effective weapon in a mother's arsenal is guilt, Mary tried to shame Jesus for disregarding their feelings.

*When his parents saw him, they were astonished. His mother said to him, "Son, why have you treated us like this? Your father and I have been anxiously searching for you."* [Luke 2:48]

The response Mary's question solicited from her twelve-year-old son is the basis for the eighth expectation God has of all teenagers -- commitment. God expects your teenager to be committed to His plan.

*"Why were you searching for me?" he asked. "Didn't you know I had to be in my Father's house?"* [Luke 2:49]

> Total commitment to God transcends all other commitments.

Jesus' answer communicates three truths. First, Jesus reveals his own understanding of his responsibility to God. Even as a pre-teen, Jesus had a desire to serve. Though he might not have completely understood the course of his mission, he clearly knew his commitment to the job was a requirement that could not be overlooked. He wanted to be about his Father's business.

Second, Jesus acknowledged his parents' right to know where he was and what he was doing. Of all the people Jesus knew, Joseph and Mary should have understood the importance of the call God had placed on his life. He was born to meet God's expectations and his parents were well aware of that fact. They knew his mission. He was the Messiah. Knowing his mission, they should have expected him to be where they found him, doing what God wanted him to do.

And third, Mary and Joseph's concern over Jesus' whereabouts was unfounded in light of their knowledge of God's call on his life. In effect, what Jesus said to his parents was, "why would you search or be concerned for me when you knew I had to be here at the temple?" Had Mary and Joseph really expected an accusation against their Messiah. Why could they not see the love Jesus felt for all men? Why would they not listen? What could they possibly fear from her son?

Pilate tried to delay the inevitable by sending Jesus to Herod. Herod was glad to have the opportunity to question the self-proclaimed "Son of God". He had heard the many tales about Jesus and wanted to see him perform one of the miracles that had been the talk of the Jewish people. But Jesus stood in silence. When Herod saw he would get no information from him, he put an elegant robe on Jesus' shoulders and sent him back to Pilate.

Mary listened as Pilate addressed the throng waiting outside his palace. "This man has done nothing deserving of death," Pilate shouted to the crowd. A flicker of hope ignited in Mary's heart at Pilate's words. "O dear God save my son," she whispered. "Please don't let him suffer when he has done nothing wrong."

Mary's hope for Jesus' release was vanquished as she heard the response of the people. "Crucify him!" "Crucify him!" They screamed in unison. With arms raised, the angry crowd pressed against the walls where Jesus was being held. This crowd would have no satisfaction short of the death of Jesus.

As she tried to think what she might do to rescue her son from certain death, she remembered Jesus' words at the Cana wedding.

"Dear woman ... my time has not yet come."

Watching the horrid events unfold before her eyes, Mary instinctively knew this was the time about which Jesus had spoken. From the day of his birth, he had been committed to fulfilling the Father's will at this moment. As he had grown and matured, Jesus had consistently advanced toward this point when his commitment would end in a job well done. There was nothing Mary needed to do for her son. His time had surely come.

> **Commitment demands that we lay down our lives for Him.**

She watched her son die that day. Innocent. Without sin and guilty of nothing but love, Jesus met God's expectation of commitment in death as he had in life. Withholding nothing, He answered God's call of complete sacrifice. Perfect. Unblemished. Enough.

With her sister, Mary Magdalene, John, and other friends, Mary stood at the foot of the cross as Jesus proclaimed his job finished. Before he died, Jesus looked at his mother and then at John. Unable to contain her grief, Mary gazed into the eyes that bore the pure reflection of God's love to humanity. Using the term of endearment she had grown accustomed to hearing, her son said,

*"Dear woman, here is your son,"* and to the disciple, *"Here is your mother."* [John 19:26b-27a]

Through tears of love, Mary saw Jesus draw his last breath. She collapsed in John's arms. It would be three long days before Mary would remember that with Jesus, hope is eternal.

> **Full commitment brings victory.**

Jesus' commitment did not end with his death. Just as he had promised, on the third day, he arose. With hope reborn and his promise fulfilled, Jesus returned to the Father where he waits even now.

In continuing commitment to each of us, Jesus is looking forward to the day when he will complete the final stages of God's plan and return to take his bride home.

**From Parent to Teenager**: Commitment to God's purposes is not an expectation reserved for Jesus alone. It is God's desire that you, too, accept the challenge of commitment. As an integral part of God's plan, you have a responsibility to complete the task God has outlined for you.

## Rules to follow:

Remember that no job assigned by God is too small or too large that commitment is not necessary.

Know that God has designed you with special purpose in mind.

Refuse to let anything impede your progress toward God's goals for your life. Stay committed to the end.

Look forward with hope to the moment you will hear the Father say, "Well done, my child. Welcome home."


Father,

Help me to be committed to your plan for my life. As I learn commitment, help me teach my child. Give me the strength I need to hold a steady course toward your goals. Help me never forget that Your plan is the best plan for my life. May my commitment to you grow daily as I discover Your will for my life.

And Father, as I go, help me love others with the unselfish love Jesus has shared with me. May my life be lived in anticipation of the day when I hear you say, "Good job, my child. Come on home."

# Chapter Nine

## God Expects Action

### {Put Your Name Here}

*I will give them singleness of heart and action, so that they will always fear me for their own good and the good of their children after me.* [Jeremiah 32:39]

One of my favorite past times is coaching girl's softball. There is nothing I enjoy more than using athletic competition to teach the lessons of life to a group of young women. Though without fail, each girl comes to the team with her own idea of accomplishment, they all eventually learn that success is measured by more than just a win-loss record.

One of the most difficult transitions for any coach is the

loss of a group of well-trained athletes to age constraints.

Such was my dilemma several summers ago. Eight of my starters had grown too old to play in our division. Left with only two starters from the previous year's team, I made a decision to draft mostly younger players. I reasoned this would give me at least one extra year to develop a team that could compete nationally.

I did not question my own reasoning until our first practice. That's when it hit me. I had to start all over again. Within the first fifteen minutes, I realized the newcomers had never been taught one of life's most valuable lessons - knowing how is not enough.

As our practice session began, I took each girl aside and asked her the most important question a competitive softball player can be asked. "Can you hit?"

One by one each girl gave the same response. With eyes round in anticipation of praise, each nodded in the affirmative. "Yes, ma'am, I know how to hit!"

Having had years of experience with teenagers, I *knew* better than to get my hopes up, but for me, knowing was apparently not enough!

As each player came to the plate, I threw enough pitches to determine if she indeed knew how to use a bat. Inside, outside, fast, slow, high, and low -- I threw every pitch I knew, wanting to give each girl the opportunity to show me what she could do. After two long hours, I stopped to reflect on my predicament. Each girl had proven my theory correct. Knowing, indeed, is not enough.

Deciding I needed to start from scratch, I had Tomeka come to the plate. I chose Tomeka to be the guinea pig because of her extraordinary physique. No more than five feet three inches, Tomeka weighed in at about seventy pounds. Eighty percent legs, Tomeka strolled up and stepped into the batter's box.

"Let me see you swing the bat one time, Tomeka," I said

as I motioned for the other girls to watch. "And swing it like you want to hit the ball over the fence." Let me mention that the fence was three hundred feet away so I had no expectation that any of the girls would be able to hit the ball that far. However, I saw no harm in wishing.

With what seemed to take more effort than she had, Tomeka picked up the bat, and gave a half-hearted swing at the air. Finished, she let the barrel end of the bat touch the ground. With a shrug, she then leaned against the bat as though she needed the support.

I held my hand up to get everyone's attention as I began my familiar discourse on hitting the softball.

"Each one of you told me she knew how to hit," I said as I looked at the group crowded around me. "Some of you even went so far as to describe to me everything it takes to be a good hitter."

I paused so each girl could mull over what I was saying. "But not even one of you stepped up to the plate and executed what you said you knew how to do!"

I looked at Tomeka since she had specifically stated that it was necessary to swing the bat hard!

"Listen very carefully to what I am about to tell you," I continued. "This is a life lesson that will one day serve you well."

I raised my index finger and pointed upward for effect. "Knowing is not enough. In life and in softball, you must be willing and able to act on what you say you know how to do."

I did not realize the impact my little speech had on Tomeka until she spoke up. Picking up the bat and stepping back into the box, she spoke with the confidence of a major leaguer.

"Ok, Mrs. Margo. But when I hit the ball over the fence, I don't want to hear one word from you about losing the ball!"

Tomeka did not hit the ball over the fence. But she did swing the bat with a determination to do so. The more she practiced the better she became. Eventually, she took on the role of our team's secret weapon. Every time we needed a long fly ball deep to the outfield, Tomeka would step up to the plate and do what she knew how to do!

> We have discovered eight expectations that God has of us - responsiveness, obedience, confidence, patience, purity, devotion, submission, and commitment. How can we put into action the cultivation of each of these eight expectations?

I, _____, Must Act!
(your name here)

Our children live in a world where they are bombarded from every direction with pictures, words, and music on every type medium imaginable to man. Bits and bytes come at them at the speed of light across computer systems linking the universe. By satellite they are able to connect up with any idea conceived by man. When they are not plugged into the world by computer or television, they create for themselves a world of sound by simply plugging their earphones into a portable media player.

Why are you surprised when your teenager looks straight through you as though you and he have never met? As you try to communicate with your child and realize his mind is light-years away, does the thought occur to you that maybe you and your teen are speaking different languages?

May I suggest that the chances are very good that your child does not know you!

My intention is not to imply that your child does not recognize the sound, inflection, or tonal quality of your voice. I don't mean, either, that your kid would not be able to identify you in a police line-up if he had to choose. After all, you are the one handing out the twenty's every other day. What I want you to understand is that your child may not *know* you. You may never have successfully conveyed to your offspring your hopes, dreams, and desires for him. He may still be ignorant of your expectations of him.

If your child does not know what you expect from him, the chances are even better that he does not know what God expects of him. Why would he know if you have not taught him?

If your child is like millions of others, his time is taken, by default, learning what the world expects from him. His growth revolves around a daily performance in accordance with those expectations.

As parents, it is our responsibility to teach our children. Unfortunately, many of us have relegated the most sacred responsibility we will ever have to the INTERNET, television, and shopping malls.

We have come to depend on our local school systems, our churches, and sometimes even our neighbors to offer guidance, support, and companionship to our offspring. We have, for the most part, given up on the idea that God has a better plan.

A study, conducted at Ohio State University and published in the journal, *Criminology*, determined parents continue to influence their adolescents' behavior even as they are being influenced by their peers. The study tracked 1,725 children for five years and verified the influence of peers, but it also determined that the parental influence remained steady throughout the teen years, showing that parents have an impact upon their children throughout adolescence.

How important it is that Christian parents wield this influence! Without your guidance, your child may never know there is a much higher authority to which he should answer. Without your active involvement in his life - teaching him as you learn - he could grow old never having realized the joy that comes in knowing and meeting God's expectations.

**Action: Response**

*"Here am I,"* said the young Samuel as he responded to the voice of God. [1 Samuel 3:4]

Do you remember the time when you responded to God - the time when you acknowledged that you were in His presence and that you were ready to listen to His voice? Share this experience with your child and talk to him about the importance of listening for God's voice, recognizing God's voice, acknowledging God's voice, and *responding* to God's voice.

**Action: Obedience**

*And the two of them* (Abraham and Isaac) *went on together* - Abraham in obedience to God; Isaac in obedience to his father, Abraham. [Genesis 22:6c]

When you as a parent set about the action of obedience to God, you will present a clear example to your child - one of obedience to a parent who obeys God, and ultimately one of obedience to God Himself.

**Action: Confidence**

*"The Lord who delivered me from the paw of the lion and the paw of the bear will also deliver me from the hand of this Philistine,"* David said. [1 Samuel 17:32ff]

Can you recall circumstances when the Lord delivered you and your confidence in Him grew? Teach your child that confidence placed in God is never misplaced.

**Action: Patience**

Joseph told his brothers, *"So then, it was not you who sent me here, but God. He made me father to Pharaoh, Lord of his entire household and ruler of all Egypt."* [Genesis 45:5-8]

Not instant rewards, but rewards gained through patient reliance on the Lord are rewards worth pursuing. Because you have learned this type of patience, you can teach your child to keep on doing what is right, even in the face of hardship and rejection, knowing that the Lord is ever-present and that in His time He will give the reward.

**Action: Purity**
*But Daniel resolved not to defile himself.* [Daniel 1:8a]
Purity is not a quality forced upon a person, but rather a quality that a person resolves to embrace. In your world and in the world of your child, impurity abounds. With decisiveness, you have chosen to remain pure and unspotted from the world. Let your child know that God expects him to make the same choice.

**Action: Submission**
Mary said to the angel, *"I am the Lord's servant. May it be to me as you have said."* [Luke 1:38]
The young maiden was amazed at the angel's message, and knew her life was about to change - her future plans were in jeopardy. And yet, she bowed in submission to God's will - not an easy thing to do. However, you know that in submitting to God, you make it possible for you to be exalted by God. Mary abased herself and God blessed her *among all women.*
What is God's will for your life? For your child's life? As you submit your will to Him, your teen will learn to do the same.

**Action: Commitment**
Jesus asked his mother, *"Didn't you know I had to be in my Father's house?"* [Luke 2:49b]
Are you truly glad when they say to you *let us go into the house of the Lord?* Have you a place of service in His kingdom? Are you committed to hiding *His word in your heart?* Are you fulfilling the commandment to *love the Lord your God with all your heart, with all your soul, and with all your mind?* Live the committed life. Teach your child to do the same!

What a delight this project has been. From start to finish, I have enjoyed every moment.

It is my prayer that because of this study you will be inspired to dig deeper into God's word to continue to discover the expectations he has for you and your children.

Margo Hemphill is the founder and director of Margo's Cargo Softball, a nationally recognized tournament softball organization for girls. She uses a mixture of humor and life to offer encouragement, motivation and loads of laughter.

Margo is available for keynotes and/or conferences in a variety of settings including corporate, civic, church and ministry.

**For more information or to schedule an appearance, contact:**

## Margo Hemphill
Phone: 601-664-0007     Fax: 601-664-0153
Email: info@margohemphill.com
www.margohemphill.com